Turn Your Passion To Profit

A step-by-step guide to getting your business off the ground

Corrina Gordon-Barnes

You Inspire Me Publishing

First published in 2012
by You Inspire Me Publishing
www.youinspireme.co.uk

Editorial: Steve Parolini, www.noveldoctor.com
Proofreading: Catherine Laurence, www.beautifulwords.info
Design: Rick Lawrence, www.samskara-design.com
Back cover photo © Rosanna Gordon

Printed and bound in the UK by the MPG Books Group, Bodmin and King's Lynn.

A catalogue record for this book is available from the British Library.

ISBN 978-0-9571689-0-9

Contents

Welcome

Welcome

So, you've found your passion. You've discovered an area of work that delights you, that you feel called to and are good at, and you've decided to step into the weird and wonderful land of self-employment. It's exciting, it's new, and the possibilities are endless.

All that stands in the way is one small challenge: how to find clients who'll pay you.

This should be easy. You're enthusiastic and ready to help others – surely people will form an orderly queue outside your door. You've gone into this field to do your life's work, not make a quick buck – surely people will see your altruistic intentions and play their part.

Sadly, it rarely works like that. Perhaps this sounds familiar: you've had a few people hiring you or coming to your sessions or classes and they've enjoyed the benefits, but it's happening slowly and you're barely able to cover your costs. Or maybe you're still waiting for that elusive first client and are beginning to wonder how you'll ever get from zero to a reliable stream of paying clients.

It's frustrating not to have a steady flow of income, but it isn't merely a matter of finances: this work matters deeply to you. It's not just your professional path, it's your personal dream. It's what you're on this Earth to do. So it's heart-breaking to hear that little voice within saying, "What if you can't make it?"

Maybe you've talked to others, read the recommended blogs and books, even taken a "how to start your own business" course or two but you feel like you're staring at a jigsaw puzzle of advice and the pieces don't fit together. On top of that, you're unwilling to adopt techniques that feel "salesy" and inauthentic; your business-building journey needs to be aligned with your values and with your integrity.

Is there a way to do business with heart? Is there a way to find paying clients that isn't manipulative – or exhausting? Is there a way to earn a decent income, without feeling like you're selling your soul?

The answer to all of these questions is a definitive yes. In this book, you'll discover how.

Ready to dive in?

Honouring your investment

If you've been beating yourself with the "I should know how to do this" stick, throw it away. There is no marketing gene. Business can be learned.

Before you studied coaching, massage, healing or whatever your passion is, you didn't know how to do it – at least, not to the degree you do now. You weren't meant to know how; it was expected that you would first need some training. You knew it would take more than intention and passion to transform people's lives, ease their pain or free them from discomfort. You first had to equip yourself with the necessary tools. Which coaching questions get someone unstuck? Which yoga asana is best for thyroid problems? Which acupuncture points relieve period pain? You invested money, time and effort in these discoveries. You studied to become proficient – indeed, excellent – at your job.

It's now time to make sure that hard work can be put to good use and you can actually help people. By engaging with this book, you're placing yourself in "discoverer" mode once again. Instead of sitting back and waiting to absorb business know-how from the atmosphere, you're actively taking charge of your venture. You're choosing to bypass struggle and frustration. You're choosing to benefit from the knowledge and experience of others who've been where you are.

Immerse yourself

Learning about the business side can be as enriching as developing your skills for the job itself. Dive right in. Self-employment holds unparalleled potential for self-development. Just as you grew as a person while becoming a competent practitioner, so too can you grow as you become an authentic, guided business owner.

It's not always an easy path. You have to find and communicate the value of what you offer and this can sometimes feel awkward or embarrassing. You have to decide the price for your services, which can trigger tenderness about self-worth. Setting your own hours and managing your own workload can feel both chaotic and impossible at times. You may feel vulnerable, hesitant to ask for help, daunted by new techniques and uncomfortable about adopting a new mindset.

It's not plain sailing but, if you allow it, self-employment can be a journey of healing. You will find a security that goes beyond your bank balance, an inherent worth separate from the prices you charge. You will be able to remedy the complications in your relationship with money, possibly breaking deep-set dysfunctional patterns. You will find a clarity of mind and a precision of expression. You will find the pleasure of communicating with others about your passion, and experience the rare joy of having people thank you for the great work you do. You will discover how much your clients appreciate your unique gifts and how generously they want to support you. You will find humility as you recognize that you're playing your unique role within a vast and thriving network of passion-led contributors.

This book signposts your journey. In it, you'll discover how to find the people who need you most, communicate your offer to them and have them say yes. As a result, you'll enjoy a steady flow of clients and receive a steady flow of income.

You probably fall into one of three groups:

- **You're brand new to business and are unsure where to start**

- **You've been trying to get your business off the ground for a while and are frustrated that your hard work isn't yet paying off**

- **You've reached a decent level of success in your business but the client flow has stalled or is inconsistent**

Pause to consider where you are.

What are your deepest hopes?

What are the reasons you chose to work with this book?

Wherever you are on the path of self-employment, now is a good time to go deeper.

If you're brand new, you're about to save yourself time, money and effort because you're working with tried and tested principles from the start. You can't do everything at once so allow yourself to enjoy learning, rather than panicking about how much there is to do. You can revisit each step when you're ready for action and everything will fall into place.

If you've been trying to get your business off the ground for a while, this book will be your trouble-shooting manual. You'll find yourself saying, "No wonder that bit isn't working; I was missing this foundational piece" and you'll have a clear sense of what to address next.

If you're old hat at this business game, you've probably got a lot of the infrastructure in place. You've got the website and the mailing list, you've built a network and have client experience to reflect on. This book will bring together those threads and help you spring clean, revamp and re-energize each aspect of your business. You'll find new ways to align what you already have in place.

Whatever stage you're at, one thing is true: you want your venture to work. You want to know that the actions you take will lead to the results you want: more clients, more ease and a healthy income. You want to feel confident that your ideas are viable. You want to let go of the panic, the frustration, the unwelcome pattern of under-serving and under-earning. You want to be clear about what to do and how to do it.

How to use this book

This book will reveal the essential mindset shifts needed to create a profitable business and it will also show you the important actions to take.

With each step, you'll encounter powerful questions that often will spark a firework show of ideas. Have a journal or notebook by your side as you read so you can record a lightbulb moment here, a flash of inspiration there. Every idea is an opportunity to grow your business.

Allow yourself to be immersed in the enjoyment of reading and then take action when you've put the book away.

As a child, you may have been scolded for writing in a book. Not here. If you have the print version, you have permission to write all over it. If you've got the PDF version, you can print out sections and scribble all over them. Then print them out again in a few months and do the same. Or you could fill a word processing document with notes in parallel to what you're reading.

When you're ready to engage actively, you'll find that each step offers a *Ready for action?* section. This outlines practical ways to implement what you've discovered. It gives you the steps to take in order to move forward with your business. As you invest time with each step, you'll gain clarity and start seeing results.

Finally, at the end of each step, you'll see a summary of the process so far. You'll see how the various steps build on each other and will experience what it's like to build momentum as your journey takes shape.

How are you?

As I'm writing this, I'm trying to picture *you*. Are you eager yet apprehensive? Committed yet twitchy? Bursting with the desire to get into action?

It's normal to feel keen to get started while also feeling unsure that you have what it takes to implement the steps you're about to learn. If you're engaged enough to pick up this book, then you're engaged enough to make it work.

Give yourself plenty of space and be patient. Until now, the *Turn Your Passion To Profit* process has been a six month journey of one-to-one or small group training. This book makes the process accessible to more people, but that doesn't mean it will take any less time to implement your discoveries. Please don't set yourself up with pressure and expect yourself to gain clarity overnight.

With the information in your hands, you can digest it in your own home, at your own pace. You can read fast, you can read slow. You can jump forward because you want to see how it all ends, and you can backtrack to be reminded of where each piece fits with the next.

And you can reach out and get support, as and when you need it.

You're not alone

Self-employment does not mean by-your-self-employment. As you're reading these words, someone in Nova Scotia or Berlin or Glasgow or Sydney is doing so too. Maybe even somebody down the road from you. You are part of an ever-growing community of people committed to receiving an income and having an impact through doing what they love.

This step-by-step programme is a living thing. It has texture and depth because of the people who have already walked a similar path to you. They have tested these ideas; they have confirmed what works best and helped me to let go of concepts that were just nice ideas.

Throughout the book, you'll encounter real-life stories that illustrate key principles and action steps. Sometimes, names and details have been changed to honour confidentiality; in other cases, you'll meet someone who wants you to know who they are – feel free to take a look at their work. You'll find them listed in the Links and Resources section on p170, along with other companies and services featured in this book.

The lay of the land

Let's look at the seven core steps within this book. The strength and efficacy of each is dependent on the previous steps.

In **Step One**, you'll learn about Connection which is about implementing a rock-solid foundation for your business and the rest of your life. You'll discover how important it is to find and strengthen this as a daily practice.

In **Step Two**, you'll identify your ideal clients, or "niche", and we'll look at the concerns that might limit your reach. You'll find practical tools for gaining clarity.

In **Step Three**, you'll discover the importance of getting to know your ideal clients and how this might look different from market research you've heard of previously.

Alert: this is the point where the action involved will make you more visible. People who reach this stage sometimes withdraw and put what needs to be done on the back-burner. Please don't. For things to be different, you need to do different things. Don't worry, you'll find that heart-to-heart research is as fulfilling as it is effective.

In **Step Four**, you'll discover how to package and price what you do so that prospective clients will love to say yes to working with you. You'll discover the crucial role of intuition and learn to take pricing out of the territory of self-esteem and ego.

Steps Five and Six are the most practical and there'll be a lot to take in. Feel free to slow down or engage with the material lightly at first and then revisit it.

In **Step Five**, you'll discover how to write promotional copy and how to speak about what you do.

In **Step Six**, you'll find the most effective, enjoyable methods for communicating with your ideal clients and you'll discover that marketing isn't as distasteful as you might have thought.

And finally, in **Step Seven**, you'll learn how to make it super-easy for strangers to become paying clients. You'll trouble-shoot your business processes, find the gaps keen clients might fall through, and discover how to fill those gaps.

You're in good company

This *Turn Your Passion To Profit* method has been tried and tested by coaches and yoga teachers, acupuncturists and osteopaths, Emotional Freedom Technique practitioners and massage therapists. It has allowed translators, editors, herbalists, Tantra practitioners and raw foodies to find more paid work doing what they love.

This is why I'm so excited to share this approach with you. When I was working predominantly with one-to-one coaching clients, I was inspired to help more people get to grips with these business principles, which led to the development of a group programme. And as the group programme saw success after success, I saw that there was another need.

Some people felt they weren't ready to invest in a programme but really couldn't afford not to learn solid business principles. I also saw that those people who were on the individual or group programme would benefit from having a written resource which brought together what they'd learned.

I wanted to ensure that talented people who want to share their gifts with others can turn their passion into a profitable business. If you are able to make life easier, less stressful or less painful for your fellow human beings, we must know about you.

The world needs your passion. It's not optional. It's an integral part of our magical, mysterious, awe-inspiring interdependent web. I need you to do what you love. You need others to do what they love. They need me to do what I love. We are here to help each other with our gifts and, in turn, be helped in meeting our own needs.

We have to move away from a world in which people sacrifice their heart and soul because they don't think there's any other way to make a decent living. There are ways – and they need to be learned.

I had to learn them. I trained at Cambridge University to become an English and Drama teacher but quickly found I didn't enjoy working within the mainstream teaching system. I handed in my notice with a pie-in-the-sky dream of starting my own school. My first tentative steps in that direction got me known as someone who saw education differently and I got asked to home-tutor dozens of local teenagers and children.

And so, in addition to doing supply teaching, I became accidentally self-employed. The more frequently I got paid for doing what came easily to me, the less it made sense to contort myself to fit a job description. The more I set my own hours, chose my clients and set my rates, the less tolerant I was of working for someone else. (You might have reached that point yourself, where you simply couldn't go back to a 9 to 5, no matter how much they paid you.)

But, while I liked being self-employed, it was quickly apparent that English and

Drama tutoring wasn't my life's calling. Then, I discovered coaching. I trained, starting picking up a few clients, and realized I needed to get more intentional about a consistent client stream. If I was going to reach the number of clients and have the level of impact I wanted, I needed to know as much about business as I did about coaching skills. If I wanted to pursue my passion as a career, I needed to learn what worked.

However, I couldn't relate to traditional Business Link workshops and networking events. Everything seemed so dry and related to cash-flow, tax-returns and legalities. Important aspects, sure, but I was more keen to discover how to find my truest purpose, stay motivated, enrol clients, discover my most authentic voice, and not let the fears eat me alive.

I realized that even if I'd had a thirty year background in sales and marketing, I would have had to learn a whole new skillset because promoting yourself as one person striving to make a difference is poles apart from corporate sales.

So I subscribed to several marketing blogs aimed specifically at one-person business guys and gals like me. I tried out their ideas, experimented with my own, made mistakes, and found what worked. I was drawn particularly to those teachers who did business differently, who did it with spirit and integrity. I saw that self-employment could go hand-in-hand with personal growth and learned how intuition and inner guidance could be my North stars. I discovered that marketing could be about serving, about honest communication, about creating bonds with the people we are here to take care of.

And this is why I'm excited to share my findings with you. I want my enthusiasm for passion-led micro-business to be contagious. I want you to find congruent ways of doing marketing so you can communicate in ways that feel natural and generous.

Because without clients, you won't get to do the thing you love. That's the bottom line. You won't have the people to do it with and you won't have the money coming in which allows you to leave less fulfilling work.

Without clients, you won't get the sense of satisfaction that you're running a proper business. Until you start getting consistently paid for doing what you love, it will remain an expensive hobby.

I've been self-employed since 2004 and have worked with over one hundred paying coaching clients and hundreds more workshop and programme participants. In the coming pages, you'll discover how success has been possible – for me, for them, and now for you.

Whether your passion is for Neuro-linguistic programming (NLP) or nutrition, writing or gardening, Five Rhythms dance or design, my assumption is that you care and you want to make a difference. By virtue of your skills and your compassion, you have something valuable to offer and you're reading this book to discover ways of reaching more people and sustaining yourself along the way.

I don't want you – or anyone else – walking around in the dark, learning from dry manuals that don't speak to your heart, discouraged by the prevalent message that claims the only way to be successful is to be manipulative. I want you to realize you can do this authentically, joyfully, skilfully, and that the money will follow.

Finally, thank you

Running your own business is by no means an easy path, despite the freedom and autonomy which often accompany it. The ongoing challenge of getting clients may have you questioning your self-worth and your place in the world; money anxieties can paralyse you and stop you from doing your best work. I'm therefore delighted that you are choosing this book as one of the ways you will support yourself in pursuit of your goals.

If you are ready to help, heal, transform and make a difference, you must not remain the world's best kept secret. We need to know about you. We need to see with total clarity that you are a solution to some of the pains and challenges that hold people back from living their fullest, happiest, best lives.

So, are you ready to find paying clients, doing what you love?

Step One
Connection

Step One – Connection

This step will enable you to:

- **Release anxiety, panic and uncertainty along the turbulent path of self-employment**

- **Establish a rock-solid foundation for your business**

- **Access your resourcefulness and a sense of being guided**

I imagine you've picked up this book with eager anticipation, excitement and perhaps some impatience. You want to learn how to create a successful business. You want to learn the nuts and bolts, the pieces that make it all work.

You're absolutely going to get that in this first step. You're going to discover bold, decisive action – but it may not look quite like you imagine. In fact, it might look a bit weird. At first glance, it might look suspiciously like treading water.

However, it is action, it is decisive, it is bold. It's just in disguise.

I'm talking about Connection.

Connection is the only place where anything truly meaningful can begin. It is vital and non-negotiable to have a daily Connection practice if you want to build a successful and lasting business.

What do I mean by a Connection practice? Connection is your way of plugging in to your greatest source of power. You might call it inspiration or inner wisdom; your higher self, best self or future self; your soul or your intuition. You might relate to the idea of the Divine, the Universe, Spirit or Oneness. You might think of it as nature, creativity, the Law of Attraction, or the vast potential of your unconscious mind.

It doesn't matter what language or which concepts you use. What's important is that you connect daily, before you even think about that endless To Do list.

You're probably already a fan

If you're a coach, you might already use a skill like "clearing" to help a client prepare for a session. You give them five minutes to clear all the stuff floating about in their mind so they can make a conscious choice about the focus of their session.

If you're a yoga teacher, perhaps you invite your students to lie in savasana for the first few minutes of a class, leaving their busy day behind. If you teach Five Rhythms dance, you probably start with a "body parts" meditation, bringing your dancers into their bodies so they can be fully present.

If you're an Emotional Freedom Technique (EFT) or Reiki practitioner, healer or massage therapist, you might begin by scanning the client's energy field, with the intention of helping to bring their system into alignment.

Even if you don't start with an obvious Connection practice, you probably do some things – perhaps unconsciously – to ease your client into the session. Maybe you exchange a few words about the weather, or offer them a cup of tea, or ask them to sit down and get comfortable.

Without preliminary acts of Connection, your client would lurch straight into the main work, possibly flustered, still fixating on the row with their partner that morning, or obsessing about the exciting email they've received. If they're off balance, your work together will be less effective. You may even feel as if you're going round in circles.

Connection gives your client a reset button. It's like setting the stage with the right props before the curtain goes up, or lining up all ten pins at the bowling alley. Connection puts everything in place, creating the optimal conditions for the work ahead.

Applying the principle to you

Alissa, a reflexologist, emailed me in a panic. "I need more clients, I need to make more money, where do I start?" She had just enrolled in the *Turn Your Passion To Profit* group programme but it didn't start for three months and she felt in such a muddle, not knowing what to do in the meantime. "Should I get flyers done, or go to a networking event? Should I start my website or get new business cards? Should I...? Should I...?"

It would have been tempting to get caught up in her panic and suggest a list of tasks, a reassuring recipe for success: do this, then that, and your business will be sorted.

But there is always the next action, and then the next. Your business will never arrive at some magical finished place. There is no finite selection of activities guaranteed to bring you the clients you want.

However, there is something much more powerful: the ability to find your own internal compass. So I guided Alissa towards implementing a daily Connection practice. She saw me after the first week of the programme. She was flushed with happiness: "I've finally put that daily Connection practice in place because you insisted it was important. And new clients keep calling me!"

This doesn't mean Alissa wasn't taking action. But the action was calmer, more considered. From Connection, she got clarity about her niche and who was most hungry for her services. She felt her eyes were open to synchronicities and new opportunities – like the chance to speak at her local mums and toddlers group. When she bumped into people she hadn't seen for a while, she felt more confident telling them about her new profession so started building a database of willing referrers. She'd basically plugged herself in to a more resourceful state and now had the foundation stone upon which everything else could be built.

How I know it works

I used to struggle with my business. Yes, I had clients. Yes, they were each paying a decent amount. But there weren't enough.

Then I hired a business mentor. I came to him when I'd hit a wall. My income was embarrassing, my client load was meagre and I was seriously considering throwing in the towel. Maybe I wasn't cut out for self-employment.

Hiring him was a brave step – a last-ditch attempt at making it work. I had a week's holiday booked just before he and I started together and sent him a flustered message via Facebook: "What reading should I take with me? What should I think about? What should I focus on, to prepare?"

His reply was powerful. "Forget about all the reading. Just sit with your heart each day."

That was the start of my daily Connection practice. At first, I did it on weekdays. A few months later, I extended it to seven days a week, holidays included, because I figured that the rest of my life deserved as much support and guidance as my business life.

My Connection practice is simple. I set a timer for twenty minutes in the morning and just sit there, connecting with my heart, noticing what comes up. I sit on my bed with a couple of cushions behind my back, cross-legged, hands on my knees, eyes closed. Sometimes I focus on my breathing, perhaps counting to ten on the breath, and then back to one and repeating, bringing my attention back when it slips. I use the Zen Lite application on my iPod because it starts and ends my Connection time with a beautiful gong sound, bringing a sense of the sacred to the experience. ("Sacred" is a quality I want to experience daily – what's your version of this?)

Invariably, some insight or inspiration comes to me. I'll get the first few lines of a blog post, or a flash of memory that I forgot to call my grandma back. I'll notice that I've woken up with anxiety, or with a huge amount of energy. I'll find I have the answer to a technical question that's been bugging me, or realize I can say no to an opportunity I've felt obliged to accept.

Just me and my heart, gently interacting, beginning the day together, connected from the start.

Choose a practice that works for you

This Connection practice works for me, but it's not a prescription.

Connection is about consciously dedicating time to that which is important to *you*, which you want to be reminded of. In order to find the practice that will be most effective for you, ask yourself these two questions:

> *What do you want to connect with?*
>
> *What version of yourself do you want to connect with?*

Here are some examples to give you a range of possibilities:

Claire, a film maker, wants to be connected with herself as a powerful female. She schedules what she calls Goddess Time. She creates funky, sensual, feminine playlists and dances with them every morning.

Charlotte is an EFT practitioner who works with severely traumatized clients. She wants to connect with a sense of safety and unconditional love so she starts her days snuggled up in bed with her two cats, stroking their fur and remembering that everything is okay. She also gives herself Reiki.

Rosanna has moved to a new city and is building up her yoga classes from scratch. She makes sure she practises yoga each day, so that she feels she's walking her talk, and also to remind herself why the effort is worth it. Because she's leading classes in addition to a full-time job, this daily practice is crucial for self-nourishment. She carves out time for her Connection practice in the afternoon, as a transition point between her job and her own venture.

Dana has massage clients booked one after the next. She sometimes feels closed in and panicked by this workload and craves space and freedom, so she gets on her rowing machine for fifteen minutes every day. She loves feeling her lungs working at full capacity and feeling the strength of her body. This Connection practice also reminds her of university days, when she was on the rowing team, a time she wants to recapture because she felt such a sense of possibility back then.

Amelia is also a massage therapist but she takes a different approach to Connection. She runs herself a bath and soaks luxuriously, surrounded by candles and gentle music. This reminds her that receiving is as important as giving and that she must look after herself too. She sometimes softly repeats an affirmation or mantra to focus her mind.

Sandie is a public speaking trainer who spends a lot of time behind the computer, writing blog posts, articles and working on her book. She knows her writing can get flat and lifeless after staring at a computer screen all day so she takes her MP3 player to the fields next to her house and cranks up dance music. This reminds her of going clubbing in her twenties; it plugs her back in to her most free, empowered self. Her writing has much more aliveness when she returns to her laptop. (She also often takes her dog on these walks and loves to connect with that sense of companionship.)

Tara recently finished her nutrition training and is starting to work with clients. She's also a busy mum and wasn't sure how to squeeze in Connection. It's important for her to connect with her children so she came up with the idea of taking a "senses walk" with them each day, stopping to smell flowers, feel the Earth and hear bird-song. This opens up her senses and also gives her the opportunity to bond with her little ones. (They love it too!)

Natalie, a coach, spends time journalling, using the practice of Morning Pages (as described by Julia Cameron in her book *The Artist's Way*) because what's important for her is accessing creativity and intuition and being able to "see" herself think. She often comes up with exercises for her clients this way.

Samantha leads workshops for teenagers, helping them to grow in self-esteem. She has all kinds of wonderful ideas for how to do this, but she can only access them when she has headspace, so every morning she sits quietly on the sofa with a cup of coffee and no other distractions, giving room to her thoughts.

As you can see, there are as many possibilities for Connection as there are people. So all that's important is exploring how *you* relate to this.

What qualities do you want to connect with?

What support do you want to access?

What kind of Connection practice might work for you?

It doesn't matter how you do Connection, as long as it creates a solid foundation for your day and you do it consistently.

But there's resistance

It's not always easy to begin the day with Connection. Do you notice a hungry desire to rush in and get to the nitty gritty straight away?

Some of that might come from fear. Fear that there's not enough time, fear that you'll miss out if you don't get to work immediately. Maybe fear of connecting with something unknown or unfathomable, or of being with your thoughts and feelings with no distractions – yikes!

And sometimes the impatience comes from excitement. You'll soon find yourself falling hopelessly in love with the business side of things. You won't be able to contain your joy. You'll wake up energized and eager to get to your marketing copy or develop your new concept.

Hard to believe? Just you wait.

The action will come

You might be tempted to skip this step. Don't.

Throughout the journey you take with this book, you'll be learning a huge amount of information and will be urged to take lots of action. If there is no strong foundation, your action will likely come to nothing, or bring results that are empty and don't align with your greatest purpose.

You could have the best recipe and the finest ingredients but if you haven't washed the saucepan and it's caked in grime and dog hair, the meal is going to be disgusting!

This is the stand I take for myself and it's how I get myself to my practice every morning, even when I don't feel like it.

Easier said than done?

You might notice extra frustration creeping in, convinced that you don't have the time for this.

I know how busy life can get. Jobs, kids, elderly parents, social demands, housework – on top of all the business steps you want to implement. There will always be activities that appear more important than Connection. You might have made previous attempts at something like this, perhaps driven by the pressure of thinking you *should* meditate, then hating every second of it, one eye on the clock. It can be hard to return to an activity that hasn't worked for you before.

You might be dubious about what a Connection practice can do for you. Isn't it more useful to put that time towards clearing your long To Do list?

> *What are your main objections to establishing a daily Connection practice?*
>
> *What stops you from connecting?*

A safe, solid foundation

> *You will never change your life until you change something you do daily. The secret of your success is found in your daily routine.*
> *– John C. Maxwell*

Placing myself in Connection each day has built my trust muscle. It has tethered me to an unconditional sense of safety, a belief that everything is – at some level – all right in the world, despite what the newspapers or my neighbours might tell me. It has brought me a sense of patience that my journey will unfold at the right pace, without the need for panic or push.

Connection has tapped me in to my intuition. Answers to my burning business questions come through this sixth sense. I have clarity about which opportunities to take up, what price to charge and the content and titles of blog posts and programmes (and indeed, this book!). It's like I sit every morning at my front door, waiting for the delivery of post, which invariably comes carrying exactly what I need to know for that day.

By moving away from panic, I can be more spacious in prospective client consultations. I don't have to grab, manipulate, coerce or pin down. I can trust that it's great if someone says yes and equally fine if they say no.

I can also enjoy more of life. I trust that it's okay to switch off the computer, eat lunch in the sunshine and meet friends in the park. (Unsurprisingly, I often seem to enrol new clients and programme participants after they meet me socially. I've learned to trust that fully living my life is a marketing method in itself.)

Still dubious?

Here are five more things to consider about Connection:

1 – All that is not from Connection is wasted

I was scheduled to do an interview with a new coach who had questions about how to start her business. She was coming over to my house but the house was a mess; I'd been rushing around like a headless chicken and had skipped my normal Connection. I didn't stop to check in and ground myself. I didn't give myself the chance to access wisdom, like I normally do when I lead a class or give an interview.

We spent a good few hours together, we recorded our conversation on my computer and then afterwards I spent another hour or so editing the audio. It didn't matter how much I edited or pieced bits together, the content was useless. I was spouting generic drivel and I could hear that I'd been thinking small, spouting clichés. The entire session was a waste – a waste of my time, a waste of her time and, crucially, a waste of the potential good that the interview could have done for other coaches. All because I didn't think I had ten minutes to sit still or take a walk and find my centre.

It's a false economy to think you don't have the time. If you were constructing a building, you'd put due emphasis on the essential preparatory phases: a rock-solid design and sufficient time to put the foundations in place. Your business has foundations too. These foundations need to be in place first, otherwise everything else is wasted.

I spent a week at Findhorn, a collaborative eco-community in Scotland, where hundreds of people live and many more visit. When you're a visitor, you're assigned to a work department – cooking, cleaning, gardening, maintenance and so on – so you're integrated into the fabric of the community and contribute to its smooth running. Every decision is made through the process of Attunement. This involves connecting as a group, connecting with Spirit, tuning in to what tasks need to be done and who feels called to do them. You practise Attunement in the main large group and then again in smaller work groups, before the morning session and also before the afternoon session.

You can imagine how much this slows everything down! But it means that what gets done is what truly needs to be done. Tasks are accomplished efficiently and enjoyably. After my experience at Findhorn, I realized a daily Connection practice wasn't optional if I wanted my business to run smoothly.

(I highly recommend participating in the Experience Week at Findhorn and immersing yourself in this powerful system of organization – see Links and Resources.)

2 – You want unlimited access

You're the business owner, the Chief Exec, right?

You're 100% in control, the person in charge. You must figure everything out and all responsibility falls on you, right?

Well, maybe. And there's another way to see the situation. You could choose to recognize that there is so much more available to you than what you can generate with your own thinking. A far greater reality can be your source.

Mark Silver runs Heart of Business and it's from him and his colleagues that I've received much of my own business guidance. He uses this analogy: it's like you're hungry and you're in one room of your house with the door shut and there's no food there and you can't see how you'll ever not be hungry because, as far as you can see, there are no food options.

But instead of feeling isolated and hungry, confined to the room you're in, you can remember that there's a whole house outside the door, and in the kitchen there's a fridge full of food and a cupboard full of food, and your house is also in a town and in that town there are shops and restaurants and so many ways to address your hunger.

This is why it's vital to connect with the bigger picture every day, as a reminder that you have more resourcefulness than you imagine.

If not for you, do it for others

Connection is an essential part of business development, not a bolt-on.

It doesn't just make things easier for you, but makes things better for your clients. You'll become an inspired channel for the products and services your clients need: articles that address their most painful challenges, recipes that nourish and heal, exercises that offer physical relief, or the right design that resonates and thrills.

If you take the short-cut and don't give yourself the optimal opportunity to receive these ideas and creativity, then you're short-changing your clients.

> *What's it like to consider that you're not totally in control? That you could benefit from help from elsewhere?*
>
> *Is it scary or off-putting, or is it a relief?*

3 – The call is incessant

You've been called to do this work. Whatever called you to your passion didn't call you once and then disappear. You are being called on a daily basis. It's a constant calling, a continually emerging conversation with whatever first called you and that requires you to be by the metaphorical phone, ready to receive the call.

You'll find there's a balance between surrendering to and receiving that call – and taking action. It's like going to a petrol station: you don't fill up a vehicle once and then forget about where the energy is coming from. Likewise, you need to be continually topped up with whatever got this vehicle of yours moving in the first place.

Your Connection practice is that fuel stop. But not all petrol is equal. You'll want to be powered by a premium fuel, one that allows you to take quality action steps and to see your calling through diligently and thoroughly.

> *How frequently do you feel you need a fuel stop?*
>
> *How can you ensure you're topping up with the highest quality fuel?*

4 – Busy days are less stressful with Connection

> *Half an hour's meditation each day is essential, except when you are busy. Then a full hour is needed.*
> *– St. Francis de Sales*

When you've got a jam-packed schedule or are facing something particularly daunting, your instinct might be to skip Connection practice. "I don't have time for this" may appear to be truthful, but it's also a convenient avoidance tactic.

The irony is that on busy or high-intensity days, it's even more important to allocate your Connection time. When you prevent yourself from taking the time to connect, you risk missing the information, guidance and nourishment that wants to come to you and that you're most thirsty for.

A Connection practice gives you the chance to step away from the task-oriented minutiae of your daily life that can threaten to overwhelm you and drag you off centre. It allows you to check in with something that's more powerful than what you, alone, can bring to the day. When it feels impossible for you to find time, that's when you most need to find time.

Make it as non-negotiable as brushing your teeth

I urge you to make Connection a non-negotiable part of every day. You do this already with brushing your teeth, right? You brush your teeth daily because you don't want the alternative; you're taking consistent action to avoid fillings and pain in the dentist chair. You don't ask yourself, "Do I want to brush my teeth today? Do I have time to brush my teeth today?" It's a daily fixture, an automatic habit.

Eliminate the question, "Do I have time to connect today?" See it as part of the fabric of your daily life, as fundamental to the process of running your business as breathing is to being alive. This way, when challenging days crop up, you'll have a solid foundation.

5 – You're part of a revolution

You may have noticed that there's a global movement towards doing business differently. You're becoming part of that. It's important for you to lean in to a daily Connection practice because of what you'll be modelling for others about how to run a successful business.

Our education and business systems appear to reward stress and fear. We may get the A grade or the promotion but at the expense of our health and well-being. For example, I got a first class English degree but over those three years, my eyesight deteriorated. Success in that context required a huge amount of reading and computer use and I accomplished this by adopting certain damaging body practices: tight shoulders, shallow breathing and eye strain. My degree rewarded those practices. My high level of myopia is a penalty I paid, so while it seemed like success to the outside world, at another level it really wasn't.

What's your version of this?

It's time for a different kind of model – where you're nurtured by your success, not in spite of it. Where you don't have to choose between health and achievement, or between time and money. I want you to feel healthy and fulfilled by the process of running a business, as well as from the outcomes, and I want others to see this about you too.

If not for others, do it for you

It's not just a revolution in terms of what others see about you, though. That's the bonus. The main revolution is for yourself.

Perhaps you've been burned by working life. Maybe your health has suffered because of previous ways of working. The approach in these pages will help you find a healthy pace and show you how to be unafraid when things go slowly. That's why we're spending time on Connection: it's vital to do first things first and put foundations in place.

My goal is to help you build a truly sustainable, fulfilling business. You'll be able to enjoy a steady pace and a sense of being deeply present, connected and guided.

How do you think having a daily practice will impact your business?

Finally, a filter

One way in which a daily practice can help is by providing a filter for you. There's a huge amount of business advice and information out there and your Connection practice can help you filter through, deciding which strategies to implement, which ones to modify and which ones to discard. It can provide you with a litmus test through which you can put any new piece of business know-how.

During the course of this book, I'm sharing the results of my own filter process. I'll show you how I focus on the core areas of marketing, the key aspects and most important principles of how ideal clients find me, thereby saving time, money and energy.

As you implement and strengthen your daily practice, you'll be able to use your own filter to do the same. As you become more and more connected, you'll find it easier to access answers to many of the key questions that show up in your business journey.

This book gives you a structure that allows you to channel your inspired ideas effectively. Whatever insights you get, through guidance, through research, through your own thinking and doing – you'll have a framework for them here.

▶ Ready for action?

In order for you to make the most of the journey ahead, experiment with and establish a daily, non-negotiable Connection practice. Allocate time each day and watch what happens next. Notice the action steps you're inspired to take. You might find yourself being drawn to a particular networking event, and when you get there, feeling drawn to speak with a particular person. You might get the title of an article you could write or suddenly feel compelled to check in with an old friend, who just so happens to be offering pro-bono website development.

Allow yourself to do business in this guided, connected way. The only way to know if it works for you is by trying.

If you have a practice that works, how might you strengthen it? If you don't, try a variety. Look back at the range of examples for inspiration. Ask yourself:

- **What do I want to connect with?**

- **What do I want to be reminded of?**

- **What is important to me?**

- **What do I want to prioritize and make non-negotiable?**

- **Is there a particular request I want to make of the Universe? A quality I want to bring in?**

- **Do I want to offer myself and my day to any intention?**

Once you've experienced Connection, notice what impact the practice has on your day.

Ask yourself:

- **What did the Connection practice add?**

- **What's the difference when I connect?**

- **What did I find difficult?**

Get curious about the days when you resist Connection. What's going on there? Do you ever doubt the usefulness of it? Do you not know how to do it? Are you worried about getting it wrong?

Here are some ways to support yourself:

- Schedule Connection in your diary as non-negotiable

- Turn it into an experiment, recording your results

- Build in accountability: tell your partner, friend or coach about your commitment and check in with them

- Make another action conditional upon doing it – for example, you have to connect before you go on Facebook or have that first morning cup of tea

- Learn new approaches: find a meditation course, either locally or online

- Acquire equipment, for example: running shoes, a beautiful journal, or a yoga mat

Permission is granted

The *Turn Your Passion To Profit* group participants are often excited at the end of the first session. One said, "I've been wanting to do daily meditation for ages but thought it was a bit self-indulgent. Now I've heard you say Connection is so important, I feel I'm allowed. I realize I was waiting for someone to give me permission!"

In case you've been in the same predicament, here we go:

You have full permission to spend time on a daily Connection practice. In fact, for your business' sake, I insist. If your partner or brother or friend says you're wasting your time, blame me – and keep going.

Let's check in

Here's what you might have spotted in Step One:

- That fear and uncertainty are normal companions along the path of self-employment and that a daily Connection practice grounds you so you feel safe, aligned and supported

- That there are tons of excuses for not putting time aside to connect, but even more reasons for doing it

- That all the nuts-and-bolts aspects of business, like pricing, marketing, having conversations with prospective clients and getting paid, are so much easier when you've got Connection as your foundation

Take a moment to gather up what you're taking from this step. Have you captured everything you want to? I invite you to reflect and make notes about your insights this far.

And let's check out

- **You know the importance of Connection**

It's now time to answer the question: who needs you and your precious gifts? Let's move on to exploring the importance of knowing your niche and defining your ideal clients. I call these your Love, Love, Money Tribe and I'm looking forward to you meeting them.

Step Two
Tribe

Step Two – Tribe

This step will enable you to:

- **Look outwards from your passion to who you're called to serve**

- **Identify those people you are a guardian angel/perfect fit for**

- **Identify the financial viability of sharing your passion with these ideal clients**

But firstly, how has it been going with the daily Connection practice?

As you move forward, it's important to maintain and strengthen your practice. Step One wasn't just a "nice idea" before the good stuff; it's the foundational piece upon which the rest of your journey will be built.

So let it accompany you and support you for the whole of this adventure – and beyond.

Who needs you?

Imagine you've discovered an amazing new recipe. You've gathered the best ingredients, you're in your kitchen, totally in your zone. You're absorbed with preparing this meal – until you think, "Hang on, people might be hungry" and you look up to see whose tummy is rumbling. You lift your eyes and focus outwards, seeing who else is out there.

In business, you need to know who's hungry for what you're serving because at the end of the day, that's how you'll be receiving your money – through people who need you.

The big shift

When you define a niche, you move into the realm of needs-based business. This is where you carefully identify a need that your passion and skills can meet.

Somewhere out there is a particular group of people who share a challenge or yearning that you are perfectly placed to address. Your challenge is to find them, communicate with them, develop relationships with them, and ultimately meet their needs in exchange for a fee that satisfies your own need – to make a living doing what you love.

I call these people your Love, Love, Money Tribe, as this term will remind you of three essential ingredients that define the niche you serve through your business.

But there's resistance!

Good old resistance again. It's a protective strategy so, rather than throwing it out, let's explore it.

Resistance to defining a niche is normal. If you feel instinctively resistant to the idea, then you're probably in the majority of the passion-led business-building population.

Here are a few reasons why:

1 – Terms like niche and target market can sound clinical and self-serving

These are the kind of words the big corporations and advertising executives use. They might appear manipulative, as if your goal is to get inside people's heads so you can fool them into thinking they need what you have.

As someone who is guided by passion and a desire to make a difference, that obviously won't sit well with you. It will jar with your values.

2 – You want to help everyone

You want to stay open, inclusive and available. You don't want anyone to feel left out. It's like you're throwing a fabulous party and you don't want anyone to feel they're not invited. You don't want to be elitist.

3 – You value diversity

You love the idiosyncrasies of people, you enjoy the uniqueness of the individual – and so you're hesitant to pigeonhole or label human beings and make them fit in nice tidy boxes. It may also feel like your ideal clients only have a few random things in common and that there's no clear thread that unites this eclectic group of people.

4 – You're anxious about narrowing

You fear that, by committing to a specific group of people, you're narrowing your reach, restricting your possible impact and also your possible income. You might feel you're putting a limit on your opportunities and that you're closing doors, burning bridges. Especially in the early days of business, you might worry that you'll commit in one direction, only to discover another direction would have been better.

It takes bravery to plant a flag in the ground and say, "This is what I do, this is who I work with" because that's about commitment. It's about declaring that you have a specific and definable expertise. When you take a stand for a particular group, then you're suddenly visible, you're in the spotlight, and that can feel scary.

5 – You simply don't know who your niche is

You don't know where you fit in the marketplace; you don't yet know the people who would most benefit from your passion and skills. This can be deeply frustrating. You might understand the value of niching and want to do it, but how can you if you don't know the right niche for you?

> *Which of these five reasons sound familiar?*
>
> *What other reasons do you have for not declaring a niche?*

Worth overcoming

Reluctance to niche is normal but it's worth tackling because a niche makes business so much easier, more fun and you can enjoy far deeper impact. It's much easier to earn a consistent income when you have a niche.

At its most basic level, a niche is a group of people who share *characteristics* and a *problem*.

So, for example: women (a characteristic) who've tried every diet and can't lose weight (problem).

It's useful to specify further. For example, women in their twenties living in Brighton who've tried every diet and can't lose weight.

This is the niche of a hypnotherapist I worked with. She saw her clients in person so the geographical factor was significant for her. If you work with clients virtually, location probably won't be an important defining characteristic.

Here's another example: stressed out mothers (characteristics) who are overwhelmed by what feels like never-ending housework (problem).

And again, to get even more specific and paint a fuller picture: stressed out entrepreneurial mothers who are overwhelmed by housework and want to sort this out because they see clients in their home.

Why they need you

With this second example, you can see not only who has a problem you could help solve (for example, if you're a professional organizer or declutterer) but also why this type of person has this need. You can begin to see how the need relates to who they are and therefore why they might be prepared to spend money to address the problem. And, right here, you have the basic requisite for a viable business: people who know they have a problem and who are willing to spend money to solve it.

As you add details to the picture of your ideal clients, you'll know who you're focusing on and you can then communicate a clearer picture to others, which is crucial for effective marketing.

Clarity will emerge over your business journey. Don't panic about not yet knowing all the details of your niche. Be patient; the clarity will come – and meanwhile, the good news is that you probably know more than you think.

You can't serve everyone

No business on this planet can serve everyone, no matter how much you might like to. You don't have the time, the energy or the resources to provide your products and services for everyone.

There's a limit to how many people you serve so it might as well be you who decides how to ration your time so you can use your energy optimally and so your efforts bring you the most fulfilment.

Declaring your niche helps people feel seen and special

I recently met a Pilates teacher and asked who she worked with. She smiled and said, "Oh all sorts, everyone." Her enthusiasm was there – but her reply disappeared into the ether and had no impact. I couldn't do anything with that information. I couldn't feel excited that she would be able to help me and I couldn't refer anyone to her.

If she'd got a little more specific and said, "I help people who sit behind the computer all day to increase their flexibility" or even "I help loads of different people, for example those recovering after injuries" – that would at least have given me more of a picture.

The vague statement, "I work with everyone" is floppy, shapeless. You could say it day in, day out, and potential clients will miss it. They won't feel spoken to or seen because "everyone" doesn't connect with them, personally.

When you say you work with everybody, the result is that nobody feels special. However, when you get specific, your communications suddenly come alive and you'll start witnessing frequent lightbulb moments where people say, "Wow, I feel you know me, you're speaking directly to me" or "Oh, you have to help my friend/mum/daughter."

Sandra Staley is also a Pilates teacher and is exploring the niche of exercise-phobes in Surrey in their thirties, forties and fifties. Clarity of niche is like holding up a missing person's poster: "Have you seen this person?" Sandra has made a great start and I've already been able to refer two potential clients her way.

Kill those carrots

I'm the opposite of green-fingered. Plants tend to die in my care, but I learned that to give carrots a good chance of growing, as with many plants, you have to thin out the seedlings.

If you plant a lot of seeds and most of them grow, they'll be competing with each other for space and nutrients. If you leave them like that, they won't have enough chance to develop and they'll fail to grow into juicy, healthy carrots.

But if you pick out and discard some of those seedlings, you give those remaining a better chance to thrive. This can feel brutal because you're killing living things but it's absolutely necessary if you want any of your carrots to make it. You sacrifice a few for the greater good.

When we translate this into the business context, it's about knowing which groups of people are going to benefit most from your attention and commitment, and then focusing your resources wholeheartedly on them.

Want to be on the radio?

There's an added bonus to defining your niche. Being specific about who you work with helps you to become well known for the particular help that you offer, and that leads to you being sought out as an expert.

A fellow coach, Beth Follini, has one of the clearest niches: she specializes in helping women in their late twenties and early thirties decide whether or not to have children. And because that niche makes her stand out, she has been sought out by *Woman's Hour* on the radio, by *The Economist* and by *Red Magazine*, to name a few.

If you're a general coach or general designer, what would the media come to you for? You need to find a particular groove so that when someone in the media needs an expert in that groove, you're the go-to person. This, of course, can provide you with excellent, far-reaching, free publicity.

A secret

Declaring a niche doesn't stop others outside your niche from finding you, and it certainly doesn't stop you from working with them, if you want to. For example, I'm clear that my niche is self-employed women yet I still get emails from men every once in a while asking if I'll work with them.

Sometimes the answer is no because the area they want support with doesn't interest me – like how to apply for jobs – but now and again I take on a male client because he's developing his business in the helping/healing realm, something that inspires me. I get to support him in defining his niche, packaging his passion and all the other steps I guide my female clients through.

When I say "I work with women", it's not because I'm averse to working with men. It simply makes it clearer to communicate with a particular section of the population that I'm most drawn to.

Defining your niche may not be as limiting as you think. Moreover, when you become clear about the main focus of your business, you become visible and stand out as a beacon. And even if your niche isn't exactly what someone is looking for, they may be attracted by your very beacon-ness! Clarity is attractive.

When I was seeking an editor for this book, I asked self-publishing expert, Joanna Penn, for her recommendations. She guided me towards Steve Parolini, the "novel doctor". Now clearly, this book is not a novel, but that didn't deter me from hiring Steve – and I doubt Joanna would have found Steve, in the thousands of editors out there, if he hadn't been a beacon for novelists like her.

Forget about forever

Throw out the myth that you have to commit to your niche for a lifetime. Take a stand for whoever you feel most drawn to now. Pursue one path with diligence. But also remember that it's absolutely possible (and sometimes preferable) to change your niche, even quite significantly, at some point down the line.

If you look at many of the large corporations, you'll see that they've done this at various stages of their business growth. Google, for example, established themselves as *the* search engine and then branched out into email, maps, phone operating systems and more.

Let's return to my earlier definition of your niche as your Love, Love, Money Tribe:

There are three elements which make for a workable niche

Nail these and you've got the basis of a solid business model. These elements are more than just business-sensible; they actually make for a dream business: one of conscious design and which is perfect for you.

If you feel stuck in the "I want to work with everyone" phase, ask yourself these three questions:

> *Within a professional context:*
>
> *Do you love everyone?*
>
> *Does everyone love you?*
>
> *Does everyone want to give you money?*

Whenever I've asked these questions on a live group call, the participants have vehemently exclaimed "NO!" to all three – especially the third – and laughed as they did so, recognizing that "I want to work with everyone" wasn't that true after all.

Let's look at each of these Love, Love, Money Tribe elements in turn:

1 – You love them

You're going to be spending a lot of time with your clients. Depending on the nature of your work, you may be getting rather intimate with them, touching their bodies, being energetically connected, hearing their deepest, darkest secrets.

What type of person do you genuinely enjoy spending time with – and in close quarters?

Do you love inspired writers? Busy mums? Expats starting their own businesses? Academics or office workers aiming for promotion? Gay men going through the adoption process? Burnt out environmental activists?

> *If you've already been working with clients, consider:*
>
> *What names appear in your inbox and you feel happy?*
>
> *If you meet your clients in person, whose faces do you love seeing?*
>
> *Who lights up your day?*

Start noticing the key characteristics of these particular people. These are people you'd help even if they weren't paying. You can't help yourself: your heart goes out to them. (Don't worry, we'll get to the part about them paying!)

This requirement of love for your clients applies even if you never meet them in person, or if it feels like your work isn't particularly intimate. If you're tutoring, catering or designing websites, you might be thinking, "It's not like I ask them about their hopes and dreams, is it really that intimate?"

Yes. When there's an energetic exchange, as there is when you're in business, it's intimate. Money makes relationships intimate. You're looking to those clients for your livelihood. You enter into agreements with them every time they buy from you.

Even if you're selling a pair of earrings, you are in relationship. There's a bond. You're interdependent: they get a particular need met by you, and you get a particular need met by them. Because of this implicit intimacy and connection, love matters.

What happens without love

I was working with a client on her marketing and explained the importance of addressing your prospective clients' pain. (We'll get to this in Step Five.) As she was thinking about how to word her website, she said, "But won't they feel offended that I'm calling them losers?"

Her response and our subsequent discussion showed us that she was seeing this group of people as weak and needy. They were unattractive in their time of challenge. She thought she could fix them or save them but essentially didn't think highly of them.

This is what *not* to do. If you feel contempt or pity for a particular sector of society, these people are not your Tribe! Avoid them, please.

If you try to create a business that serves a group you have judgements about, your lack of genuine respect will come through in your communications and push prospective clients away. Trust that other businesses will serve these people with positive regard, and allow yourself to be drawn to people you can love *especially* in their times of greatest need.

When your marketing comes from this place, it's authentic and heart-felt which is much more attractive to new clients.

"But I love everyone!"

This is what Louise de Caux, a Tantra teacher and *Turn Your Passion To Profit* participant, was grappling with. The focus of her work was around finding the beauty in everybody and seeing through to the core of the human being in front of her, so how could she name preferences?

We can certainly find ways of loving lots of people, and anyone can potentially be a useful client for our own evolution and maturity as a practitioner. But why not make it easy for yourself? Why not find the clients you are most energized working with?

Louise – and others on the programme – realized they had an assumption that working with clients and making money had to be hard work. Running a business couldn't possibly be about playing with your favourite kinds of people all day.

I give you full permission to find the people you have the most fun with. This is one of the huge assets of self-employment – you choose who you spend your time with. (And if you're committed to there being struggle, you can always find an extra client or two who are challenging and press all your buttons!)

2 – They love you

Even if you got stuck on the first element, even if you feel like you love everyone equally, you need to check that these people love you. And I mean – *really* love you; they cannot wait to speak with you, to do business with you. They think you're their guardian angel, dropped from the heavens.

This might sound like an ego stroke – and of course it does nurture your self-esteem – but it's much more than that. This element is important because it affirms that your uniqueness is precisely what a group of people needs.

It's about being acknowledged and appreciated exactly as you are – and that makes a refreshing difference from previous experiences you may have had, of working for a company that is constantly appraising you and giving you targets for improvement.

When you know you're loved by your client group, you can relax, assured that you are perfect just as you are. You can speak with your most genuine voice and your idiosyncrasies will delight them.

Tad Hargraves teaches marketing to hippies and writes about guerrilla gift-giving, organic farms and offering free hugs on the street. Naomi Dunford also teaches marketing and has a bold, no-holds-barred approach; one of her case study examples involved a sex shop and a vibrator. If you're in either of their Tribes, you don't just tolerate the hippie and the straight-talking, you're hungry for them.

Likewise, your natural style is what your true Tribe are hungry for. If you feel you have to adapt and amend yourself, your path of passion quickly becomes drudgery and you'll find yourself longing for your previous job.

People who love you love to tell others

This element does wonders for your referrals too because people who love you will rave about you to their friends and colleagues, which of course brings more clients your way.

If you work with people who don't value your unique blend of talents, their lack of appreciation will impact how you respond to them. You might even deliver a half-hearted service (literally, half-hearted) and who would they refer to you after such an experience? Instead, they might tell potentially ideal clients that you're not that great.

In my early days, I certainly worked with clients where the requisite "click" wasn't there. I didn't do my best work and they didn't get the best of me. Don't waste time here. There are enough people who will be thrilled to discover you, just the way you are.

What great love matches have you had?

When have you felt this reciprocal love and appreciation between yourself and a client?

What has it been like when the love wasn't there?

How might it affect your business if you made these two "love" elements non-negotiable?

What would your business be like long-term if you didn't make these two elements important?

3 – They want to give you money

You may be able to spot your ideal client a mile off if you look *only* at those first two elements. These people love working with you, you love working with them, but when it comes to the payment, you encounter a block.

Perhaps they say they love what you offer and they want to exchange with their skills, paying in kind. Maybe you design a book cover for them and they repay you with Shiatsu sessions. There's certainly a beautiful sense of community interdependence with this kind of model, but for this to be a business that lasts, there must be a healthy incoming stream of actual money.

You might be inundated with the reciprocity of massage and yoga classes and home-baked cookies, but if you can't pay your mortgage, your rent or your bills, then your sense of relaxation will fade fast. You'll feel nourished in many ways but you'll have no roof over your head, no insurance and no electricity.

In our current societal set-up, we have to pay for certain elements of our lives with hard cash. Your landlord or mortgage provider is unlikely to buy into a skills swap, much as you might like them to.

A great love match isn't enough

When you want to turn your passion into a genuine business, people you love and who love you aren't destined to be your clients if they aren't willing and able to pay a fair price for the service or product that meets their need.

Yes, your business could still help them if you offer some of your expertise for free or at low cost. I have many helpful articles on my blog, for example, that are accessible completely for free by people who may never become paying clients. You could design a business model that provides bursaries or scholarships for a certain percentage of people.

It's important to keep free or discounted services distinct from those you offer to your core Love, Love, Money Tribe. They, after all, allow you to pay your bills and stay in business.

Business can be as generous as a charity, but this book isn't called "How to get your charity off the ground". The only way you can offer services pro-bono within the business context is if you have enough profit to allow for that generosity.

Notice any discomfort?

Julie, a *Turn Your Passion To Profit* participant, kept attracting prospective coaching clients who didn't have any spare cash. After a number of months of this same pattern, she realized what was going on. She was from the East End of London, considered herself working class and had made up all kinds of stories about what middle-class people with money were like. She was concerned they'd think less of her because of her accent and background and that they'd expect more than she could deliver. She felt more comfortable coaching people on a low income and yet people in this group weren't able, or willing, to pay her coaching rates.

For ages, I resisted the advice that I needed to work with people who had the money to pay me. I held the perspective that people with enough money weren't the kind of people that I wanted to work with.

It was utterly exhausting and disillusioning. It also turned out to be a fiction. My Tribe do have £1,500 for private mentoring, £900 for a group programme, or £40 for a book. They have the money and they want to invest it in support. Your Love, Love, Money Tribe will too.

So please place at the heart of your business the concept that there must be people who have the money to pay you what you want to earn. If you look honestly, you'll see that this is the only logical way for you to be in business.

And if you're not convinced there's money out there, spend five minutes in the middle of a busy high street or shopping centre and watch thousands of pounds worth of purchases flowing all around you. It's a powerful antidote.

Wait, there's more...

Not only can your ideal clients afford you but they love to give you money. I don't want you to beg people to pay you. That just feels icky.

I want you to move away from believing that people will begrudgingly say, "Oh okay I'll part with my money if I really have to." That's not going to bolster your sense of self-worth and affirm you're on the right path.

Instead I want you to have the experience where your new clients say, "I desperately want to pay you because you're amazing and I know that you can help me so much." Imagine that. Literally, right now, run that little movie in your mind and notice how it feels.

This feeling is something you'll experience over and over once you nail this definition of your Love, Love, Money Tribe.

▶ Ready for action?

It'll be an ongoing journey to discover which group of people are ripe for you. You can gain clarity about your Tribe from so many different angles. With this book, I've included two bonus visualizations. These audio tools can be found at *www.youinspireme.co.uk/tribe-clarity* and your password is: angel

▶ ▶ Audio 1

Firstly, listen to the *Meet Your Ideal Client* visualization. Imagine you only get to work with one person for the whole of your business life. A scary concept I know, especially if you resist the idea of niche because it feels limiting.

I frame it this way because I know the power of a death-bed question like: "If you got to help just one person, who would it be?" It cuts through the clutter, the vagueness, and frees you from apathy; it connects you to your very highest purpose, the focus that will give your working life the most meaning.

Above all others, who would you serve?

From one to many

Once you've got a sense of one person calling you, extrapolate from that and know that there's a whole Tribe of this kind of person calling you. Suddenly, a niche doesn't feel so restrictive!

▶ ▶ Audio 2

The second visualization is called *Whose Guardian Angel Are You?* This concept has been a popular reframe for those who fear niching makes them elitist. The premise is that you are here on this Earth for a reason and that there are certain people who need you. This is about letting your intuition guide you towards who is calling you and then diligently answering your unique calling.

If visualizations don't do it for you, feel free to use your favourite Connection practice and simply ask yourself, "Who do I most want to serve through my business? Who do I feel called by?"

Make notes about who you meet in your visualizations and reflections. What are their characteristics? What are their main challenges or needs?

Now, put your findings to the test. Do they line up with all three Love, Love, Money Tribe elements? Do you love these people, do they love you, and do they have the money to pay you?

If you draw a blank and this part feels challenging, please don't worry. We're just getting started. The Love, Love, Money Tribe concept will evolve for you over time. The real-life examples throughout this book might spark some realizations, as might your encounters with people over the coming weeks.

Spot the obvious

As you make your notes, be aware it's often the obvious we don't spot.

Very often, members of your Tribe look like earlier versions of yourself: people a little further back on the track you've been walking. For example, Nicola Marshall has adopted three children and through her coaching practice now helps other adoptive parents to get through times of doubt, struggle and despair and find the courage to be highly effective parents.

Often, your Tribe consists of people you've always associated with (for example: creatives, academics, horse-lovers, twins) and this group feels so much like home, you can't see that it's not normal and natural for others to associate with them. In fact, you might be surprised to discover that others can't connect with your Tribe. For example, it was a revelation for me to hear that some people are scared stupid of working with teenagers, whereas that relationship comes easily to me. They were the first Tribe I worked with and I didn't understand why fellow coaches called me brave!

This is one reason it helps to seek coaching, mentoring or buddy support when getting to know your Love, Love, Money Tribe. It often takes someone else to point out the obvious.

Another way to hone your Tribe is to use the process of elimination. This helps counter the myth that you want to work with everyone. Ask yourself: Who *wouldn't* I work with? People approaching retirement? Hippies? Children? Royalty? Corporate professionals? Earth mothers? Men deciding whether to have a vasectomy?

It's not that you don't like them. It's not that you're being discriminatory. They're just not who's calling you right now.

Trust that each part of the world will be taken care of by someone; you don't have to answer everyone's needs. In fact, by trying to help everyone, you'd actually be abandoning your post. Along with the *Whose Guardian Angel Are You?* visualization, you might find this passage provides a helpful nudge towards claiming your Tribe:

> *Instead of trying to be responsible for all the problems in the world, we should take on what we love and care about. There's no separation between the two, and there is no hesitation, no self-doubt. This will help us develop great faith that others are taking care of their piece. It is very important that we share, not only our merit, but also the responsibilities. Somehow we have to relieve ourselves of the enormity, which is so debilitating.*
> *– Paul Hawken (Environmental Activist and Entrepreneur)*

Some examples

One of my clients had a sense that her Tribe might be women over fifty wanting to start their own business but she wasn't sure which characteristics were important. Gender? Age? The business aspect? She wondered if it mattered whether they were married, single, separated or divorced.

So she started a Tribe Spotting list. As she watched TV, she ran an internal commentary, saying things like, "Ooh, he's too old" or "Ah, she's patient and friendly, I wouldn't want to work with grumpy people", and started to get a sense of which qualities and characteristics she was most drawn to. When she bumped in to a middle-aged lady at the Post Office, she created a whole back story for her: she imagined the lady was married and lacking the confidence to do certain things but that her husband would support her when she knew what she wanted. My client was creating fiction but if it were true, this woman would be precisely her Tribe! She realised which characteristics mattered and which were red herrings.

Let's say you have an amazing connection with a forty-year-old male accountant who's going through a mid-life crisis. The next time you have a similarly strong connection with someone, you can check if any of the same characteristics are there. Are you drawn to accountants, regardless of gender? People going through a mid-life crisis, regardless of profession? Or career-oriented men, regardless of age?

Keep playing with your understanding of your Tribe, using the formula: shared characteristics plus shared problem. Who are those people whose lives you can make easier, less stressful, less painful? Which clients would give your working life the most meaning, the greatest sense of purpose? Eventually, you will find a Tribe with whom you feel completely in your natural element.

Here are a few examples:

- **Women who've found their passion and want to make a difference but don't yet know how to make that pay the bills (mine!)**

- **Busy London women who've dieted all their lives and have never kept the weight off**

- **Adoptive fathers who haven't yet found their role and are feeling disconnected from their partners**

- **Academics who want their essays published in languages they don't themselves speak**

- **Working mothers who want to feed their children healthy food but don't feel they have the time to home-cook**

- **High-achieving professionals earning £50,000+ who've woken up and thought, "Isn't there more to life than this?"**

- **School teachers who suffer from repeated migraines**

- **Women desperate to have children, for whom conventional fertility treatments haven't worked**

- **Male survivors of rape who are craving a healthy relationship with their own sexuality**

- **People approaching retirement who feel anxious that they'll be losing their identity**

- **The teenage children of divorcing parents whose schoolwork is suffering as a result**

- **New fiction writers who've decided to self-publish but don't know where to start**

Important: Your niche doesn't have to be unique. People often stress about having to find out "what hasn't been done yet". That's not the question. The question is: who, specifically, are you most drawn to help?

Muriel Bauer, a psychotherapist and life coach, was gaining clarity that her Tribe were women and especially mums who are feeling invisible. She was concerned, however, that lots of other practitioners were set up to meet this need. Did that mean she needed to choose another niche? No, quite the contrary. It simply suggests that there are a lot of mothers at home who feel invisible and need to regain confidence. There needs to be a community of professionals to support these women, and Muriel can take her unique place within that community.

I went to a new hairdresser. He'd set up in Cambridge on a busy street called Mill Road, known for its many salons. I was curious as to why he'd set up here, when there were already so many hairdressers. His answer: "I set up here *because* there are so many salons." He's been successful because he spotted an area that required multiple practitioners.

Spend time here

Allow yourself plenty of space to reflect. Go through a list of people you know – friends, clients, colleagues – and identify which characteristics and problems attract you.

Also, make a list of who you are and the challenges you've faced and overcome. Often, your own path is what makes you the ideal match to help others through similar journeys.

As clarity starts to come, spend time thinking about what makes your passion the perfect fit for this group of people.

Let's check in

Here's what you might have spotted in Step Two:

- **That there are certain people you prefer working with and, since you can't serve everyone, it might as well be you who decides how to ration your time**

- **That defining a niche is nowhere near as restrictive as you feared – in fact, it can be liberating and lead to exciting new opportunities**

- **That you need to focus your business services on a group of people who can pay you, otherwise you'll never have a profitable business**

Take a moment to gather up what you're taking from this step. Have you captured everything you want to? I invite you to reflect and make notes about your insights this far.

And let's check out

- **You know the importance of Connection**

- **You know the importance of defining and claiming your Tribe**

It's now time to answer the question: what do these people need?

Let's move on to exploring the importance of doing research with your Tribe. Don't worry, this is much more pleasurable than it sounds as it involves hanging out with people you love and who are grateful that you exist.

Step Three
Research

Step Three – Research

This step will enable you to:

- **Identify the key difference between an eager paying client and someone with objective interest**

- **Discover an enjoyable and effective way of building a needs-based business**

- **Get into action with heart-to-heart market research**

How are you doing with defining your Tribe?

Each step of this *Turn Your Passion To Profit* business-building journey acts as a stepping stone for the next. Having a daily Connection practice remains crucially important. If you find your practice slipping, or if it's not yet established, revisit Step One and re-commit to implementing a strong daily practice. It's the foundation for everything else and, most importantly, will help you to feel safe and centred as you progress with self-employment.

Here in Step Three, let's get to know your Tribe more deeply and discover what they need.

With the previous step, we focused on overcoming uncertainty about defining your niche. But being able to identify your Tribe doesn't happen overnight. What's more likely is that you've moved from saying "I work with everyone" to accepting and understanding that your Tribe is a smaller, more focused group. Whatever clarity you have about your Tribe will help you with this next step, and this step will in turn help you become clearer about who your ideal clients are.

A foundation for success

This next step is market research, or hearing the need. Your business will be successful in large part because you decide to base it on a foundation of research.

With research, you'll determine if your Tribe is a genuine market. That's why this step comes before you get into marketing.

When I started doing research, it transformed my business. You'll discover how I do it and why I do it and you'll see that research is not a dry exercise in statistics and doesn't need to involve standing in the street with a clipboard (unless you like that sort of thing, of course).

Firstly, some background. When I started as a coach, teenagers were my niche. Along the way, I found myself being called to work with their mothers and with other women who were struggling with what to do with their lives. From there, I realized the clients who most excited me were those who had inspirational ideas but felt blocked from turning them into reality.

I realized I needed to know stuff. I needed to know what it was like for these women to be in their situation. I needed to know what kind of support was already out there, to see if there was a gap in the market that my support could fill. I needed to know if what I wanted to offer was something they would pay for. And I needed to know how to find and reach these women.

"Needing to know stuff" is simply another way of saying "needing to do market research".

How to do that

I emailed my existing contact list (a mixture of friends, relatives and previous colleagues), explaining that I wanted to find out more about what it's like to be a woman who has an idea that would make a difference in the world but feels blocked from taking it further. I explained that I'd be interviewing one hundred women and I gave the research a title: the Inspirational 100 Project.

With each interview, I'd be asking about three core areas: (1) their current situation and its challenges, (2) what support they were already getting, and (3) what support was missing.

I also wanted to run a few ideas past these women: which formats suited them best (did they like online products? would they like a weekend residential course?) and which titles they got excited about (for example, *Fail Is Not A Four Letter Word* or *Kickstart Your Venture*).

I wanted to ask which kinds of phrases they might type into a search engine like Google because I wanted to make sure I knew what they were thinking when they sat down to look for help. How would they phrase their needs?

I wanted to know where I might find them – which magazines they read, which groups they were part of, which forums they chatted on.

I basically wanted a thorough knowledge of my market's needs and the best ways to access other women like them.

Each interview would take only thirty minutes and the participant could choose whether the questions were answered via phone, in person or by email.

Finally, I wanted to thank them so I offered each participant a thirty minute coaching session in appreciation for their time and insights.

Not quite dry statistics and clipboards, huh?

What do you notice about that research process?

Take a pause and notice your reaction. Perhaps it sounds exciting – like a project you can sink your teeth into, a fun way to connect with those people you've identified you want to help.

One woman on my *Turn Your Passion To Profit* programme said it "sounded like a lot of work!" In part, that's true. My version involved one hundred hours of one-to-one contact time, plus write-up, plus finding the women to be interviewed.

However, it didn't feel like a slog because it was time spent hanging out with my Tribe (who I love, after all). Moreover, I felt confident that it was saving me time in the long run – because it was giving me a thorough research base to build from. Time spent here would ensure that I got the packaging and pricing of my services right, that I created meaningful and appropriate marketing messages, and that I targeted my marketing efforts in the right places.

And research doesn't need to involve this many hours. It's up to you how much information you want. Most of my clients find a half dozen interviews with their Tribe gives them enough of a base to move on to the next steps, and they keep going with the research because it continues to be enjoyable and beneficial.

You might wonder why you can't just find and use relevant existing research. The answer is that what I'm advocating is a different type of research. It's not statistical, it's not an analysis of consumer habits that you'd find published in Marketing Week. It's heart-to-heart research where you're hearing people's deepest needs with your own ears, not reading them second hand.

Why is research effective?

Let's identify what was so effective about this research, so you know the key wisdom to take away as you plan the research stage for your business.

The first great thing about doing research is:

1 – Research stops you from thinking you're psychic

We can't – and shouldn't – assume that we know how people feel and we can't assume we know why people want or need certain things. It's important to see things through the eyes of our prospective clients.

I love the story of Alex Bellos, a maths writer and author of *Alex's Adventures in Numberland*. He is often asked what his favourite number is but he doesn't have one. The concept is absurd to him – that people would have an emotional connection with an impersonal concept. Yet, when he asked around, he realized that he was unusual. He found that most people do have a favourite number and that this choice is often passionately held. This puzzled him. Since there was almost no research on favourite numbers, he decided to do some himself and so launched a website – *www.favouritenumber.net* – in which tens of thousands of people have entered their favourite number and explained the reasons for their choice.

That's an extreme version of research; you'll probably be doing a lot less work than that, but for the same purpose. Although your clients are often similar to you, or walk familiar paths, you can't assume you know their perspectives or reasonings. You might be an anomaly!

One *Turn Your Passion To Profit* participant was setting up an artisan bakery. She could have just thought about her own outlook, asking, "Why do *I* spend £2.10 on a loaf of bread from my local bakery when I could spend 80p and get it from a supermarket?" She'd rather support a local enterprise than a giant store. If she were only considering her own reasoning, she'd target all her marketing with that slant.

The majority of her prospective clients, however, might not care about supermarket politics. Perhaps they want better quality bread because they get irritable bowel syndrome, or experience acne, or feel lethargic when they eat mass-produced, high-additive bread. It's not only useful to expand your understanding of your Tribe's reasons and motivations, it's critical.

Once you stop trying to be psychic, and hear others' perspectives, three great things happen:

1 – You can confidently package and price your product or service because you know the format in which your Tribe would like to receive your services and also how they make their purchasing decisions.

2 – You can create a marketing message that speaks your Tribe's language.

3 – Your confidence gets a boost. You may have been hoping people need what you're passionate about but it's energizing and affirming to actually hear them say they do.

It's a relief not to have to be psychic. Embracing research offers you a refreshingly easy way to start your business because you're not immediately launching yourself at the world, assuming you have all the answers. Additionally, a perspective that states honestly and openly, "I need help" is welcoming and will attract your Tribe.

2 – Research means your business will be financially viable, with a customer base, not just a fan base

What's the difference between a customer and a fan? This might feel like a simplistic question but pause and consider.

Picture a market place (after all, what is "marketing" but a repurposing of that three-dimensional place where we meet to buy things?). Imagine a real-life, bustling city market where at one of the market stalls you see a market trader who's selling bananas.

Now picture a woman wandering through the market. She sees the stall and comes over and says enthusiastically, "Oh wow, bananas are my favourite fruit, they smell so good, I love what you're doing, you're amazing!" Then she walks on past. She's not hungry; she has no need for a banana. Although it's been a nice boost for the market trader to see her enthusiasm, no money has changed hands.

Time passes and then a man approaches; he comes straight up to the banana stall and says, "I'm hungry" and points to the banana. "Oh that's what I need – I'll buy that." And then he hands the trader his money.

You may be thinking that the difference between a customer and a fan is that money is involved. This is true, but the key question is: *why* is money involved?

The woman may be far wealthier than the man, she might be able to afford to buy every banana the market trader could sell for the next five years but she's not going to become a customer if she's not hungry.

When there's a need, money is likely to follow. If what someone's offering promises to take a person's hunger away, it's worth paying for. In other words, the product or service is worth more to the customer than the money sitting in their pocket or bank account.

The core difference between your fans and clients is that your clients have a hunger. They have a need.

But surely fans are useful too?

Of course, the woman may come back another day and buy a whole bag of bananas. She may tell lots of people about the banana stall. She might turn out to be precious to the business as a future client or referrer, but right now, all we know is that she's a fan. She admires the concept, but she doesn't need the products or services.

It doesn't matter how amazing your work is if you're not connecting with people who have a need, or a hunger. You can bask in all the praise and acknowledgment in the world but unless someone is paying you, you're not truly in business.

Don't ignore your fans – love them, cherish them, treat them with deep respect and gratitude – but remember: if you're relying on your business to pay your bills, you need to focus on having *clients*.

Research is about discovering who needs you so you can focus your business efforts on them.

Which brings us to:

3 – Research helps you create a needs-based business

By focusing on needs, you switch your business position from "I'm trying to make you buy this thing, isn't it amazing, let me push this on to you" (which is how a lot of businesses *do* operate, unfortunately) to "Let this be the painkiller you're looking for."

It's a shift to a gentler place, where there's no pushing or coercion, no pleading for sales. You recognize you are there to meet needs that already exist. You become a beacon for those people who are already searching for ease, for relief, for a solution to their challenges.

You want people to recognize your work not just as admirable but as helpful and useful. You want to communicate that your services meet genuine needs and hungers in people who are willing to pay to get those needs met.

Do you feel that shift?

What would it be like to feel you had a genuinely needs-based business?

How would you then approach your business activities?

No-one needs herbs

Very few people, if any, wake up thinking, "I have a huge need for herbs and I'm willing to pay good money to get them." (Well, unless you're talking about the illegal kind!)

However, someone might wake up thinking, "I've had a horrific night's sleep, I've been sleeping badly for a while, it's been affecting my concentration, my work is suffering, I feel terrible. If only someone could help me with that, I'd certainly be prepared to part with a little cash for relief."

So, if you're a herbalist, make it your mission to research the "disturbed sleep" need – and likewise for the other conditions that your herbs can help with.

Similarly, it's unlikely that a parent will suddenly think, "I need to find a forest schools practitioner." But they might think, "I live in a flat on the seventh floor and my kids don't seem to be connected with nature. I'm scared they're getting attention deficit because they're only used to TVs and computers and four walls. I don't want that for my children. If only someone would come along and provide a fun way to get my little ones connected with nature, I'd happily pay them and be so grateful."

So, again, if you are a forest schools practitioner, make it your mission to research the "children disconnected from nature" need.

You'll then start tapping into a genuine market and can begin packaging what you offer to best meet those needs and market those packages accordingly.

It's a harsh truth but nobody specifically needs coaching, story-telling, Qi Gong or whatever it is you're offering. They don't need those tools. But they do need solutions that those tools can provide.

Identify a motivating hunger and you have the potential for a needs-based business. This is what sustainable profitability is based on.

4 – Research helps you with packaging and pricing, with your marketing message, and with knowing which marketing vehicles to use

In the research stage, you're creating a foundation for these next three steps.

By the time you've done a fair amount of research, you'll be familiar with your Tribe's needs and you'll find those meeting points between what they need and what you're passionate about offering.

Each of these meeting points provides an opportunity for you to package your services so they come across as true solutions and your confidence in those matches will come through in how you market what you offer. In research, you'll hear the exact phrases your Tribe members use to communicate their main challenges so you can use their language in your promotional copy and in conversations with prospective clients.

And as we're talking about marketing, here's the fifth reason why market research is so valuable:

5 – Research *is* marketing

I set up my Inspirational 100 Project as simple market research. I imagined it would give me the information I needed to position myself and attract new clients. It did meet this goal, but I didn't realize that it would *directly* generate clients.

I started noticing a pattern: a large percentage of the women I was interviewing went on to become paying clients or workshop participants.

In fact, one in three of the women I've interviewed have gone on to become paying clients. To use classic marketing lingo, that's a 33% conversion rate. Considering that most marketing strategies – like emails or flyers – have a conversion rate of around 2%, my market research turned out to be a very effective strategy.

And the research wasn't even set up as a marketing strategy!

As useful as all this research is for deciding what you offer, at what price, and how to market it, remember that every bit of market research *is* marketing in itself. Even though at this stage you may not think you're doing marketing, you are getting (at the very least) attention from prospective clients.

Every time you speak with your market, you're marketing. When I told people about my research project, I was essentially making a public announcement, declaring, "This is what I'm now doing. These are the people I care about. Are you one of them, or do you know someone who is?"

Every time someone encounters your research, whether they see it broadcast in your Facebook status or on a poster, or whether someone tells them about it, they're starting to associate you with the people you serve and the needs you meet.

Imagine, for example, that Susie sees a flyer at her local health food shop which reads: "Julie is doing research for her new coaching business and is looking for women in Brighton who are in their thirties and forties who've lost a sense of who they are in the world, and what they have to offer." Assuming that Susie fits that description, what impact do you think that flyer would have on her? She'll see herself and her situation mirrored back to her and will associate Julie, the coach, as being positioned to address her needs.

A less threatening way in

Marketing, when done directly, can be off-putting. Most of us don't like feeling we're being sold to.

Imagine someone comes up to you in the street and says, "Hi, I'd like to tell you about my reflexology business, do you have a minute?"

What would your reaction be?

Now imagine someone is standing there and says, "Hi, I'm doing research with local people who experience migraine attacks. Do you get them? If so, could you help me out? The conversation takes ten minutes and I'm offering every participant a 10% discount voucher for a session with me; I'm a reflexologist who specializes in drug-free treatment for headaches and migraines."

Would your reaction be different?

You might find the second example feels more open and inviting. You might feel curious and happy to help.

One of the women who took part in my Inspirational 100 project – who later went on to become a *Turn Your Passion To Profit* group participant – said she'd found it an easy way of engaging with me and my work. She said:

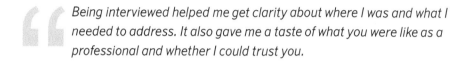

> *If I'd booked a consultation with you, I might have felt pressured to pay you back for your time, or like I was obligated to you in some way. The way you did it, once I'd had my thank-you session, the transaction felt complete. There was no unfinished business. There was no pressure for me to have any more contact with you – so when I did choose to enrol on to the programme, it was because I wanted to.*

Another said:

> *Being interviewed helped me get clarity about where I was and what I needed to address. It also gave me a taste of what you were like as a professional and whether I could trust you.*

As it happens, she also went on to invest in the *Turn Your Passion To Profit* group programme.

Busy and cynical

You might not have liked the idea of the reflexologist approaching you with her research. When you imagine yourself as a busy shopper, you might feel harassed or think, "Well hang on, there must be a catch."

Great to notice. People may be suspicious of your intent, so plan your research with awareness that your Tribe might feel overwhelmed or cynical or resistant. Explain clearly to people why you're doing what you're doing and how it's of benefit to the research participants too. Also, be prepared that a lot of people will say no, and remind yourself that it's not a reflection on you or the worth of your work.

This brings us to a paradox. Although market research can work like a dream as marketing, *do not* approach it this way. People will be able to smell a hidden motive if you deliberately make your research a cunning marketing ploy.

Instead, approach it purely as research – and then be prepared in case people ask how they can work with you. (Have those answers ready – more of that in the next step.)

Research: from "why" to "what" and "how"

You've read the five main praises I want to sing of this research stage. Now it's time to prepare for action. When it comes to the nitty gritty of conducting your own research, *what* should you ask about and *how* should you do it?

You know how a magazine sometimes features stories with Before and After photos? Begin your research by finding Before pictures. In other words, what is it like for your Tribe before they encounter you?

Symptom spotting

Symptoms are what let you know you have a need. How do you know you need to go to sleep? The symptom is tiredness. How do you know you need food? Your tummy rumbles.

> *What symptoms do your Tribe experience before you come along?*

Margaret Hiley is a translator. Her Tribe are academics who want their work translated from German to English. Before they meet her, here are some of the symptoms they're likely to be facing:

They're busy and feel particularly anxious, concerned that their work won't reach enough people and have the desired impact. They feel frustrated, impotent or limited. They're dragging their feet, delaying their enrollment in a conference because that would involve dealing with the translation issue. Perhaps they've spent money on computer software that promised to translate their work but found it was inadequate.

Their world before you enter

You want to know what primary symptoms your Tribe are experiencing before you offer to help them with your services. You want to know the details, so rather than just knowing that your Tribe procrastinate, consider what that looks like. Do they read blog post after blog post rather than writing their own? Do they organize their CDs alphabetically, or fritter time away commenting on their friends' photos on Facebook?

Do your Tribe's issues with body weight mean there are places they avoid? Do they miss out on key events or experiences? What other areas of their life do these issues impact?

You'll find there are *chronic* symptoms that build up over time. Then there is an *acute* moment which brings their struggles to a head. For example, one of my Tribe suffered from a chronic sense of frustration and lack of clarity. When she was thrown into the spotlight at a local networking event and someone asked what she did, she got embarrassingly tongue-tied. With another the acute turning point came when her partner said, "You've got an expensive hobby, not a business" and she suddenly determined, "I've got to sort this out."

Ask your research participants: Out of 10, how bad does your situation or pain get? What is bearable and what's unbearable? What can you handle yourself and how do you know when you need help?

If they use a phrase, like "mid-life crisis" or "burn-out", ask when they started using that phrase to describe their experience. Was there a particular incident involved?

You want to understand in depth what their life is like. As a result, you're likely to feel an extra large dose of compassion for your Tribe. This has the added bonus of solidifying your desire to help this group of people. It affirms why you're their guardian angel.

At some point, when they're out there in the world, your Tribe will start to recognize these symptoms in themselves and consciously or unconsciously begin searching for solutions to make these symptoms go away.

When your marketing speaks about these symptoms, and when there's a clear correlation between your service and how it will take these symptoms away (or at least lessen them), that's when things click and your Tribe decide they want to explore working with you.

Research Focus 1

Discover your Tribe's symptoms. Find out what it's like for them right now. What's frustrating, what's painful?

After setting the context for what you're researching, here are the types of questions you could ask:

- **How's it going for you?**

- **What are the most challenging aspects of your situation?**

- **How does this impact the rest of your life?**

- **What have you not told anyone (or many people) about?**

- **What do you wish someone would understand, without you having to explain?**

- What would be the cost of staying in this situation another year?

- What would it be like if this never changed?

Make a list now of what kind of symptoms you're expecting to hear.

Great. Now throw that list away! It's an interesting exercise but the point of doing research is to hear *their* answers so you don't have to be psychic. As you listen for your Tribe's symptoms, you might be surprised at how different they are from what you were expecting.

Research Focus 2

In the Before picture, you also want to find out what your Tribe have already been trying, and how well that's been working. In other words, if you didn't come along, all passionate and wanting to serve, how would they attempt to meet their needs?

This is more traditionally known as assessing the competition, and although I don't advocate thinking of it in those terms, it's important to know what other services and products meet the same needs you're targeting. You also want to discover what activities your Tribe are distracting or anaesthetizing themselves with, because the money they spend there (whether it's on shopping, drinking, holidays, or entertainment) could instead flow towards a more effective solution to their challenges – namely, your service.

Here are some useful questions to ask your Tribe:

- What kind of support have you been getting for this?

- What books or websites have you read that address these challenges?

- Have you hired anyone to help you resolve this?

- Who do you know that might be able to support you with this?

Research Focus 3

Hearing about existing solutions will naturally spark your curiosity about the next focus area, which is: what do they feel has been missing? Where have other services and products fallen short in meeting their needs?

Here are some useful questions:

- What did you get from reading that book, or working with that person?

- How directly did you feel that support addressed your specific situation?

- What support that you desire or need isn't available?

What you hear will be useful for how you package your service (we'll explore this in the next step). If you keep hearing that other services didn't work because they were too time-consuming, or inconvenient, or didn't go deep enough, then this will help you identify how your service will be a better fit for their needs.

You'll start seeing the gap in the market. Let's take the example of Amanda Galati, who's a designer. She's been researching with her Tribe of conscious entrepreneurs and has been asking them about branding. She's discovered a pattern in that they've either tried to design a logo themselves, or have had a creative friend give it a go, but they aren't using the logo because it doesn't resonate. It might look good but it doesn't reflect them and their business. Amanda's specialism is that she "receives" the logo design using a variety of Connection practices, after having consulted with a client. Hers is an intuitive design that is more likely to resonate with the client. This is her unique position.

You're not asking these questions in Focus 2 and 3 to prove you're better than anyone else, but to discover how you might be able to fill a gap.

Time to get psycho

As you hear these answers, you'll be encountering the *psychographics* of your Tribe. What a great word!

In Step Two, we defined a niche as a group of people who share characteristics and a problem. You discover the psychographic characteristics when you start having a deeper, more intimate understanding of your Tribe. Psychographic features are those that can't be seen: people's hopes, their fears, how they relate to the world, what motivates them, what blocks them, what's in their psyche.

My Tribe, for example, share a psychographic characteristic of wanting to make a difference. Yes, I help women who need business know-how, but that's not the full picture. *Why* do they want business know-how? My Tribe have a very particular motivation for this: they want their business to make an impact in the world. Lots of people want business know-how for completely different reasons that just wouldn't interest me.

I discovered the importance of this psychographic by interviewing lots of women and finding that the ones I clicked with and cared about were the ones where this characteristic was present.

Be alert for the psychographic characteristics that excite you, inspire you, and cement the first Love aspect of your Love, Love, Money Tribe. This is another tool for finding your unique position as a service provider.

Craft your research questions so you can discover the deeper aspects of your Tribe and subsequently so your business can meet those needs in a more powerful way.

Research Focus 4

Mention a few of your service ideas and see how they're received. Which formats do people get excited about? Get a sense for how possible solutions might suit them.

For example, you might say:

- **I'm wondering about offering this in a two-day residential course, all accommodation and food included; how does that sound?**

- **In addition to one-to-one training, I could lead a group programme – would you like that?**

- **How would an e-product version suit you?**

- **What if I could bring the fold-up massage table to your home?**

There's a chance you'll be disappointed and hear that they don't like the sound of some of your cherished ideas, but it's better to hear that at this stage rather than after you've booked a venue, designed a product, or written all the publicity material. Your Tribe's reactions – their preferences and aversions – will lead you to offer services they're hungry for.

Time to bring in money

There's a chance that money is your sticking point – that money, along with marketing, seems far removed from a heart-centred business. Does that feel true for you?

It was true for me. I was brought up by beautiful parents who told me that money can't buy you happiness. I made friends with people who didn't earn a lot of money but were happy; I gravitated towards those who were committed to changing the world, not increasing their bank balances.

I had to address my relationship with money and ask whether this perspective was serving me. I still wanted to be happy and make a difference, but I wanted to receive a healthy income too. Were these goals mutually exclusive? I discovered they weren't. In fact, when I allowed money to be important too, I found I could make *more* of a difference.

For example, I had the funds to invest in self-publishing this book. It's deeply fulfilling to be able to pay a professional editor, a designer, a proofreader, a printer, a web developer and an assistant. By shifting my perspective on money, I have become more able to contribute to others.

This is a big topic, worthy of another book (which I've already started writing!) but suffice to say, I do the work I do, helping women earn good money doing what they love, because I know what it's like to struggle with this area. I understand the inclination to conveniently forget about the money aspect of business and I know the energy drain of giving without knowing how you will receive.

I don't want that for you. Money is just like any other part of your business, built from the groundwork of Connection. If you find money a sticky subject, lean in to your Connection practice even more deeply.

> *If I hadn't mentioned it, would you have thought to ask your Tribe about money?*

In the early days of my own research, I avoided questions about finances. I felt they'd taint the conversations. Now, when I ask my research subjects about money, it brings us into a refreshing intimacy. Let's explore how you can do that too.

Research Focus 5

Bottom line: you need to know if people would be willing and able to pay for what you'll be offering. Please don't ignore this piece, even if it feels hard.

I do suggest avoiding *direct* money questions, however. In my experience, it's not so useful to ask, "What would you pay to resolve this?" or "How much should I charge for this service?" You'll hear numbers that are inflated because your research subject is keen not to offend you, or numbers that are deflated because your research subject is trying to secure a future bargain.

Instead, look to draw comparisons with where your Tribe have spent money in the past. You want to establish what they consider valuable. You could compare with parallel services. If you're a coach, you might ask how they've known it was time to hire a therapist, counsellor or mentor in the past. If you're a Pilates teacher, you might ask how much they've previously spent on yoga or Tai Chi classes.

Ask questions like:

- **When did you last pay for professional support?**

- **Where do you spend money easily?**

- **How much have you spent on massage/counselling/workshops in the past?**

If you keep hearing people say that it's a waste of money to pay out for professional support, you're not interviewing your Tribe. There are plenty of people out there who are delighted to pay for services that will help make their life easier, less painful or more joyful. Find them!

"I can't afford you" often isn't true

When I did general life coaching, I had a great client who ended our work together earlier than we'd both have liked because she said she "couldn't afford" coaching. That sounded fair enough: she was a mum of two little children and wasn't earning much money.

I later found out she'd spent £500 on a Tantra weekend for herself and her partner. If I'd researched mums like her and discovered they'd happily spend money on support that strengthened their relationships – and if she'd been my ideal client and I felt coaching would help her with that – then that's what I could have focused on conveying to her.

Be transparent when asking these questions so your research subjects don't feel you're prying. Explain that you want to ensure your business is financially viable.

Ask:

- **What brings you to a buying point?**

- **What's been the final straw that led you to spend money in the past?**

- **What tips you over the edge, from tolerating a problem to taking action to solve it?**

- **How do you decide it's time to pay for support, rather than managing on your own?**

Find out what your Tribe's motivation is for spending money. The answers you hear will help you to price what you do (Step Four) and communicate the value of your services (Step Five).

Research Focus 6

In this final area of research, find out how your Tribe search for solutions to their needs. Ask:

- **What would you type into a search engine?**

- **Whose opinions and recommendations would you trust?**

- **On which online forum would you ask a question about this?**

- **Which magazines do you read? Which websites do you visit?**

The answers you hear will help you to target your marketing efforts, which we'll be exploring in Step Six.

How do you actually do this research?

Research should not be a chore. It should not feel laborious. You love your Tribe and this research gives you an excuse to hang out with them. Hooray!

(And if that doesn't feel like an appealing prospect, it's time to check whether this group of people really *are* your Love, Love, Money Tribe. Recognizing and properly analysing your reaction to conversations with these people could save you lots of time, money and effort in the long run.)

Assuming you've identified a prospective client group that you do love, ask yourself, "How do I *want* to connect with them and hear about their needs?"

You might decide to do your research one person at a time. You might email out a questionnaire or create an online survey. You might ask research questions on social media, or set up a small focus group in person or by teleconference.

Be creative, think outside the box. A massage therapist named Allison invited half a dozen neighbourhood women to her home, provided scones and tea, and pasted huge sheets of paper to her wall, to capture their responses. With public methods, you might not get such honest responses (group dynamics can sway responses) but a good group setting can provide a wealth of ideas because one person's answer might spark another's.

If your business is geographically located because you sell physical products or because your services are likely to be offered predominantly in person, consider researching on the streets or door to door. (You may need a licence and identity card to do this in your area; check with your local authority.) One option is to find local groups that could invite you in to conduct research with their members. For example, Tricia, a foot health practitioner, set up a research slot at a local retirement home.

Whatever method you use, you'll be asking people for their time and openness so make sure they understand why their input is valuable. Also, consider offering a thank-you.

What to give in return?

Offer something equivalent to what you've asked of your research participants. If they've given you ten minutes of their time, don't overwhelm them with a free full-day workshop; the exchange won't feel balanced. Instead, you might enter them into a prize draw to win a place at that full-day workshop.

Choose something that makes sense for your business. Rather than "Thanks for taking part, here's a chocolate", make your thank-you relevant to what you offer. (Obviously if you offer chocolate-making workshops, that would be the perfect thank-you!)

My thank-you of a thirty-minute coaching session gave people a taste of what it would be like to work with me one-to-one. This is one reason it had such a high conversion rate as an accidental marketing strategy.

Audrie Reed is a film producer whose passion is to capture people's stories and create short documentary-style films. When she ran her research project, she offered a thank-you of half an hour of scanning photos or editing film, giving potential clients a taste of her expertise. Lorraine Burwood, a parenting coach, offers a free e-book, *The 7 Secrets Of Successful Parents*, as her thank-you.

When I was designing my workshop, *Fail Is Not A Four Letter Word*, I did another research project into relationship with failure, and everyone who took part was entitled to a 10% discount on the workshop price that they could use themselves or pass on to a friend.

When you approach your thank-you this way, you tap into the triple-win involved in this kind of research process: not only are you finding out about your Tribe, but you're giving them something back for free, and simultaneously marketing by giving a taste of what you offer.

> *How could you set up your research thank-you so that it's also effective marketing?*

But how do I find my Tribe?

Once you're happy with your research questions and you've thought of a relevant thank-you, you're ready to speak with your Tribe. But how on Earth do you find them? How are you going to spread the word about what you're doing?

Think about your favourite ways of spreading the word about exciting events or important issues. Do you phone people, or a put a shout-out on Twitter? Do you design a flyer, or ask a well-connected friend to spread the word?

Translate your natural communication preferences into your research preferences. Here are some options for finding research participants:

You might:

- **Phone or email your friends**
- **Link to your online survey on social media**
- **Print flyers**
- **Tell people about it at events**
- **Write about it in your newsletter**
- **Mention it on your website or on the back of your business cards**

Activate those methods you would normally use to make contact with people when you've got something newsworthy to share. When I started research, I didn't have a newsletter and Facebook and Twitter didn't exist so don't worry if you don't yet have much infrastructure set up – there are other ways!

Find a megaphone

Amplify your reach by asking others to pass along your request. This is one of the best leverage strategies – it's a way to do less work yourself and get greater results.

I met Denise Duffield-Thomas at an event. We chatted for ages, we clicked, and she was so enthused by my work that she emailed her entire network about my research project. She was well-connected and from this one person, I was contacted by dozens of women who totally belonged in my Tribe. Many of the women who came via her went on to become paying clients.

The clearer you can be about who you want to reach, the easier you make it for others. Denise was already hanging out in the kind of communities – both online and offline – where lots of my Tribe were. So, when she heard me talk about wanting to find inspirational women, she knew she could help.

Some people, like Denise, are natural megaphones. They love spreading the word about cool things.

So ask yourself:

- **Who likes spreading the word?**

- **Who might know lots of people in your Tribe and be able to access them with your research request?**

- **Which mailing lists might feature you?**

- **Which magazine could mention your research? (This is a less immediate but potentially effective strategy. You can create an article or short announcement that asks readers to email you if they're interested in helping you out.)**

Every community has a hub. An online forum has a moderator. A magazine has an editor. An event has an organizer. A group has a leader. This hub person can be your megaphone. They have the potential to make your life a whole lot easier because their opinion is already highly respected by the people you're wanting to get in touch with.

Make it safe

Petra Schlitt, a coach, was concerned that her Tribe wouldn't want to admit they had a problem. Rather than advertising that she was looking for men having a mid-life crisis, she decided instead to announce, "I'm interviewing business men in their forties about how they deal with stress." Then, when they get into a conversation with her and are reassured that what they say will be held in confidence, she can go deeper into the aspects that might feel less socially acceptable.

When Petra listens and cares and shows she understands and that what these men feel is quite normal, her Tribe are likely to feel a great sense of relief – and so her research is actually generous, a service.

Depending on which field you're working in, you might get a better response if you appeal to the aspects of your Tribe that they would happily identify with – for example, talk about "busy mothers" rather than "mothers who feel they can't cope".

▶ Ready for action?

Your assignment in this step is to talk with your Tribe.

If you feel definite about your Tribe, you can make a big song and dance about it, like I did with the email announcement. If you're still testing the waters, put feelers out quietly and have one or two initial conversations.

If you're feeling torn between two distinct Tribes, you could turn this into a competition and frame it like: "I'm exploring which groups I most want to serve through my business and so I'm asking: who needs me the most?"

Make notes now about:

- **The format your research will take, e.g. 30 minute interviews**

- **How you'll find willing participants who are in your Tribe, e.g. email your contacts**

- **What incentive you'll offer, e.g. a thank-you session of the same length**

- **How you'll reassure them about confidentiality, e.g. you won't share their answers with anyone else**

- **How you'll amplify your reach, e.g. megaphone people whose help you could enlist**

Then take a look at your draft ideas and check:

- **Does it sound fun? Is this you in your natural element? Will you look forward to it or does it feel like a chore?**

- **Does it feel effective as market research? Are you getting close to your Tribe? Are you likely to receive responses that are useful in how you package and price your offerings? Are you likely to hear your Tribe's needs and be able to construct a marketing message using their language?**

- **Does it have the added bonus of being effective marketing? Is it associating you with a particular niche? How does the thank-you aspect feel? Does it help your Tribe engage with you and what you offer?**

If your research project feels solid, then it's time to start the research. Be open to hearing information that will be valuable for the next few crucial steps of your journey.

If you've been dreading getting into action, I hope you now feel that the pressure is off. You're not going out there to sell, you're going out there to be curious, explore and discover. You'll be meeting interesting strangers whose lives you can make easier – both ultimately and through giving them space to reflect now.

You might start your research with a flurry of excitement. My hope is that you continue doing research throughout your business journey. Any time you find someone new who fits your Tribe, you now have an opportunity to connect with them more deeply, rather than thrusting your business card or website at them.

Let's check in

Here's what you might have spotted in Step Three:

- **That there's a crucial difference between fans who just love you and clients who love paying you**

- **That a needs-based business is more likely to be a profitable business**

- **That market research is basically a good excuse to spend time with a group of cool people**

Take a moment to gather up what you're taking from this step. Have you captured everything you want to? I invite you to reflect and make notes about your insights this far.

And let's check out

- **You know the importance of Connection**

- **You know the importance of defining and claiming your Tribe**

- **You know how to do heart-to-heart research**

It's now time to answer the question: how can you best meet your Tribe's needs?

Let's move on to exploring the nuts and bolts of packaging your passion so that it's a perfect match for your clients, and pricing your services so people happily say "Yes!"

Step Four
Package and Price

Step Four – Package and Price

This step will enable you to:

- **Match your passion with the needs of your Tribe**

- **Create a way of channelling your passion so it's a comprehensive solution**

- **Set prices that feel right to you and to your ideal clients**

Quick check: are you still strengthening your daily Connection practice? As you move forward with this book, you might notice you feel overwhelmed. The critical voice might be chattering away in your ear, asking why you haven't done everything already. You might be tempted to tell yourself you're not good enough or haven't been doing enough. Connection can quieten that voice and offer more compassionate ways of being with this process.

No-one said it would be easy

As you start to become comfortable with research, you'll notice what a beautiful foundation this gives you. Hearing the needs of your Tribe will get you excited about packaging what you do to meet those needs.

Don't stop researching; stay focused on gaining more clarity about your Tribe's deepest, most acutely felt needs. These are the needs your Tribe are prepared to take action and spend money to meet.

The research stage is the first time I've asked you to take action that others will see. You may have noticed an urge to quit, to hide, to not fully engage. You may have felt like staying in the ideas stage because it seems safer there. Lack of clarity can be frustrating. Action can be terrifying. All your doubts and anxieties can surface and threaten to overwhelm you.

If you notice any of this going on, lean in to the support you have around you. Your coach, your buddies, your friends, your partner. Tell them you need a little help. If you've noticed you're plodding and dragging your feet, tell them you need a kick up the backside. If you've noticed you're frantic, chaotic, a whirlwind of ideas, tell them you could do with some grounding.

Tell them what you need and let them help you get on track.

Please don't abandon your journey because you feel alone. Reach out, find allies. Self-employment isn't always easy, but you're doing precious work so do find ways of sustaining a healthy level of inspiration, energy and momentum.

Anyone want to play Snap?

Your brain has been hard at work. Firstly, thinking through your Tribe. Then, gathering research information. Your grey matter is growing a database about the needs of the people you're best placed to help, even if it currently feels like a tiny database.

You also know a great deal about the other side: your passion, your area of expertise and talent.

With the guidance in this step, you'll start bringing these sides together to find correlation and overlap. It's like playing Snap. "They need this" – "I love to do this" – "Snap!"

Snap Solutions

"Snap" occurs in business when you find how your passion is the perfect solution to your Tribe's needs. Your clients want solutions. They want to reach a destination, they don't care which route or vehicle gets them there. They aren't specifically looking for hot stone massage, Reiki or Alexander Technique. They want solutions to the needs they've been carrying around for days, weeks, months or even years.

Ultimately, your business model will consist of a variety of Snap Solutions. You may have heard this described as multiple streams of income.

First, however, I'm going to walk you through a process for getting clear about one Snap Solution, one package. It's best to work through one package at a time, getting clarity before you go on to the next package. You can duplicate this process again and again as you build your business, but for now, let's get you solid with one.

Here's a three-step process for packaging and pricing what you offer:

Stage 1 – Intuitive packaging

Bring to mind one person who is a good representative of your Tribe. It might be a person you spoke with in your research, or a paying client, or a practice client. Make a note of their name and what their main challenges are.

For example: *Jane is a typical member of my Tribe. She has a difficult relationship with her body and feels anxious about her appearance. She feels ashamed and thinks that no-one is there for her. It seems there's no support or acknowledgement of what a battle it is between how she sees herself and how she wants to see herself.*

This is your starting point. Always start with your Tribe and their needs.

The next step is to ask: How could those needs be met? In what format could support be packaged, to be the ideal solution to those needs?

Now, where did I put that intuition?

You have a lot of information. Now it's time to trust your intuitive sense of how to put it all together.

Where do you feel your intuition?

It can sometimes seem hard to grasp. Is it through the top of your head, your gut, your heart or the ether? Does it come to you in images or words or feelings?

Put your hand on a part of your body or move physically to represent an intuitive posture to remind yourself that this is where your answers are going to come from. If you're not sure how you feel your intuition, make it up. (Building a strong link with your intuition may be a useful focus of your daily Connection practice.)

As you answer the following questions, keep in mind that your goal is to come up with the ideal format to meet this person's needs. Don't yet think about how much you like the idea of providing this package or how much it might cost. You'll get to that in subsequent stages. For now, we're going for the uncensored version, the optimum prescription, discovered from your intuition.

Best format

Q1. What are this person's primary needs?

Example: *Someone to hear her without judgement, and give her space to put into perspective where she currently is in her life.*

Q2. Knowing this, for how long does this person need support? (Remember to answer from your intuition)

Example: *Between nine months and a year.*

Q3. How frequently do they need support?

Example: *To start with, weekly for six weeks. As she becomes more comfortable and more confident, it could shift to fortnightly for a four month period. And then when she shifts into the next gear, it could be monthly.*

As the answers to these questions come to you, notice that if they are truly coming from your intuition, they will feel resonant. They will purr, they will feel right, they will click – because they make sense to your heart.

Q4. What key phrases or titles would suit this format?

Example: *The first stage is Release. Then when she's working with her beliefs and set patterns of behaviour, that's Acknowledge. Once she understands "Ah so this is what happens when I get out of bed in the morning", then she can change. So the final stage is Design. So it's a three-stage journey which lasts around nine months: Release – Acknowledge – Design.*

Q5. How long would each session be?

Example: *60 minutes.*

Q6. What is the format for each session?

Example: *By phone.*

Remember: at this point, it's not about *your* preferred format. It's about what is going to be most effective for meeting your Tribe's needs. What will they prefer, given the nature of their needs?

For example, phone work might sound appealing but deep down you know your Tribe crave physical touch. If you trust your intuition, you will know that the optimal format would be in-person. Or perhaps your Tribe would feel safer and allow more intimacy if they could call from the comfort of their own home, without having to dress up and leave the house. In this case, their ideal format would be by phone.

If in-person is a given (for example, if you're offering bodywork), then ask yourself: would they prefer sessions at their place or yours? You might also check in with your intuition about whether one-to-one or group work is the better format.

Your intuition will draw on all the information you've been receiving from research, as well as from your previous experience.

Q7. Does the format require additional support (e.g. interim support between sessions, email support, laser calls, a buddy system, sessions recorded, documents you send, extra bonus features)?

Example: *She can contact me by email or text between sessions so there's a degree of hand-holding but it would have limits. She'll be growing but not growing dependent on me.*

Q8. What's the over-arching theme of this format? What title would you give it?

Example: *Well it's about freedom. Learning to live as she is, rather than as someone in a box where no-one sees the real her. I don't want her to get to the point where the anxiety is so deeply embedded and she's in such a desperate, severe state that psychotherapy is the only option. What's coming to me is: The Freedom Journey: Save Yourself From The Body Anxiety Box.*

A starting point

Perhaps you've been struggling with this piece for a while. You know what you want to do and with whom, but you haven't been sure how to put it out there in the world.

The packaging and pricing step will help you decide how to share your passion so that it meets people's needs and is a great fit for what you most enjoy doing.

You may be surprised at how much clarity comes and at how near the surface your answers are. Remember, you know a huge amount about your Tribe, both from experience and from research. The package you create will make sense to you because you've tuned into the wisdom that's already there, available within you.

Can't I just say "I offer coaching"?

You might be thinking that this process makes life more complicated than it needs to be. "I offer massage, why can't I say that and ask the prospective client how many sessions he wants?"

This is a common question. Here's why that doesn't work:

As you claim your Tribe, get to know them deeply and help them as a professional, you're becoming an expert in this niche. When someone goes to see a doctor, they know what hurts, they know what kind of relief they're hoping for, but they shouldn't be expected to know the route to take to get there.

A doctor doesn't say, "How many tablets would you like to take? How long would you like to take them for?" She says, "Here's a seven-day course of antibiotics: take them three times per day and you'll feel better." When you're feeling unwell, there's great relief that comes when the doctor knows the solution. (Of course it's important that the client also feels empowered about their own journey and sees themselves as an expert in their own life.)

The *"free yourself from body anxiety"* example I used above belongs to a coach named Jacqueline Beall. She knows her Tribe. She knows about their journey. She knows how long people need to commit to get results and she knows the level of support that feels engaged but not overbearing. I have faith in her and I'd refer people to her because she has that confidence and expertise.

Resistant again?

You may notice some concern. "Ooh I don't know about being an expert, giving a prescription."

This is the same part of you that would have resisted declaring a niche. The part that doesn't want to put a stake in the ground, to be visible, to be out there. This is the part that lacks confidence and would rather stay under the radar. It's tempting to hide behind the "I work with everyone and however you want it is fine" approach because it's passive; it avoids responsibility and the possibility of failure.

This part of you probably also believes deeply in the resourcefulness and wisdom of others, and is concerned that by taking the expert position, you undermine the expertise of the prospective client.

This is understandable; you've no doubt seen people manipulating their position of authority. Many so-called experts have stripped people of their own empowerment, encouraging a "just follow me" attitude. I know that's not what you want – and that's not what this is about. I want you to stand fully in your integrity, knowing what you know and what you're good at, without compromising the autonomy of others.

Two experts can exist at the same time. You are the expert in your skill area (your coaching, your massage, your healing or whatever it may be) and the prospective client is the expert in their own life. Owning your own expertise actually allows your client to do the same.

Tailor-made

You may not be keen on this concept if you think it means your talents are being squeezed into a one-size-fits-all solution. Even within a clearly defined Tribe, each person needs a uniquely different approach, right?

Yes, absolutely. This is what your initial consultation stage is for (we'll explore this further in Step Seven). A consultation is your chance to hear the individual prospective client's needs, match them to your standard solution, and assess if your service is best exactly as it is or with amendments.

Each package can be tweaked or tailor-made for the unique individual, but it's important to have a clear package to start from. You'd probably find it bizarre if a restaurant didn't have a menu. Sure, you can have a conversation with the waiter about what's available in the kitchen and decide to "hold the olives and substitute the pine nuts" but it makes more sense to be presented with a pre-determined list of dishes you can adapt, rather than the waiter expecting you to create a brand-new recipe!

Ultimately, you'll have a range of options to suit different needs. You'll be able to channel people towards the package most suitable for them. Let's say you go on to develop five packages. Once you've heard a person's situation, you can suggest the appropriate one.

Perhaps someone really wants your full service but can't afford it. You might look at developing a "mini" version, where someone on a lower budget could benefit from, say, the three most crucial elements. I saw an example of this recently with a trainer who'd put together a special "essentials" version of her full programme, to make it more affordable for a particular section of her audience.

Nothing is forever (unless it is)

It's important to note that declaring, "This is what I offer" doesn't mean you can't work with people in other ways. Nothing is set in stone. You might create a four-session package now and then a few months down the line decide an eight-session or two-session package would work just as well, or better, to meet your Tribe's needs.

Remember that idea of being a beacon? It applies here too. When you're clear about your package, your communications are clear. That makes it easier for people to approach you and say, "I'm attracted to what you do. A twelve-week programme feels too long for me; do you have other options?"

At that point, you have a decision to make. If a prospective client is asking for a process to take less time than you feel it needs, fall back on your expertise and your experience. Don't say yes in order to make the sale and then under-deliver. If you truly believe it's going to take at least nine months to achieve the desired results, stay true to that.

Likewise, if you think it would only take one session to get this person to their desired solution, then that's your package. Focus on the impact of your work, rather than how long it takes. Look to your intuition to find a title you might give a quick-fix solution. Would you call it a laser, kickstart or radical transformation session?

Don't string people along. Don't add fluff to bump up the price. Come up with a package that is an effective solution – neither puffed up nor made too lean – that you can stand behind.

What if support is needed more sporadically? Here's a conversation I had with Joy Haughton when she was starting out as an osteopath:

Joy: Do you think everyone who comes to you needs some kind of package? Or does it work to have some people just turning up for a session?

Me: What would you prefer if you were the client?

Joy: It would depend on my situation. Preparing for a marathon, I could well want a package with after-race care but if I'd just woken up and tweaked my back and was in agony, I'd want it sorted out that day. A client like that isn't interested in a package, they want immediate first aid.

Me: Great. It's easier for people to identify that something meets their needs when you give it a name. So you could call your drop-in service your Emergency Service. This is useful for two reasons; firstly, they can identify that it would meet their immediate needs. Secondly, it's much easier to market. At networking, you'd mention, "I also do an Emergency Service so if you ever meet someone who's woken up and tweaked their back, send them along to that."

How I know it works

A few years into self-employment, I was wondering how to package my one-to-one coaching services. I was doing one-off sessions, a number of workshops and a few special offers but nothing felt particularly sustainable.

I knew a lot about my Tribe and I had one idea after another about how to help them, but I wasn't coming up with anything new and useful, so my mentor (Jason) helped me get centred in my heart and my intuition.

I tuned in to the question of how to package my coaching and Jason asked, "How long would a session be?" My heart gave me the answer: 90 minutes.

As a one-to-one coach, I was confused; that felt far too long for a session and I thought, "Well this is stupid, let's go back to logical reasoning. My heart obviously doesn't know what it's talking about."

Then Jason asked, "And how many people are you speaking with at a time?"

That's when it clicked. I realized that one thing my Tribe wanted, in order to get their needs fully met, was to be in a supportive, like-minded group environment. That was the birth of the *Turn Your Passion To Profit* group programme, which turned out to be one of the best things I'd ever done for my business and for my clients. I still repeat the group programme several times a year, plus it led to more structured one-to-one coaching, as well as this book. If I'd censored my intuition when it first spoke up, you wouldn't be reading these words!

Get out of your way

As you go through this process, be open. Throw away the obvious packages and listen to your intuition to find what your Tribe really need. It might feel daunting to let these answers come but they'll lead you into a greater sense of safety and success. Keep your preconceptions out of the way; the packages you come up with might look quite different than you expect.

This is not yet the time to think about whether it's the service you thought you would be providing, or about what price you'll put on it. The danger of bringing those filters in too early is that they stunt the process. When you notice your mind chiming in with, "Well this isn't how I normally work" or "This is going to be too expensive, no-one is going to pay!", put those concerns to one side for now and focus on getting clarity first.

Once you've got a thorough, unabridged prescription of a package that meets your Tribe's needs, it's time to move on to:

Stage 2 – Who or what is needed to make this a comprehensive package?

You've come up with a package that would be great for your Tribe. Now it's time to put yourself back into service-provider mode. As the person who has to provide this service, ask yourself: Does this work for me too? Does this format suit me? Does it play to my strengths? Will I enjoy working in this way?

No?

If certain aspects don't feel like a match with your way of working, you can recommend and refer to other people and services. Joy, the osteopath, gives a list of computer programmes to her clients who are experiencing Repetitive Strain Injury (RSI). She doesn't want to develop software herself and doesn't need to because she knows there are quality products that already meet the appropriate needs. She might even decide to become an affiliate of one of those software companies and earn commission each time a client buys the software. An extra income stream like this can be a win-win-win.

Lisa is an artisan baker. She wants to focus on baking but she knows some of her Tribe want to learn those skills themselves so she co-opts a friend who is keen to run bread-making workshops. Her friend in turn spreads the word about placing monthly bread orders with Lisa.

A fully comprehensive package for my Tribe includes helping them develop an online presence but I don't want to design websites so I recommend my own web developer Adam Kayce and also Laura Roeder's *End Your Website Shame* package (see Links and Resources).

> *Who might you partner with?*
>
> *Where might there be a reciprocal/financial benefit to you, which would also benefit your clients?*

Procrastination busting

Procrastination often happens when we need to delegate something, learn a new skill or step out of our comfort zone.

You might like the sound of the new format that's coming to you but feel daunted because it's unfamiliar. Maybe you're used to coaching in person and your intuition is telling you to put together a phone package. Maybe you're comfortable teaching raw food workshops but are now being guided to offer ongoing meal-planning and whole-life mentoring.

There may be a learning curve involved in offering your services. You might need to learn how teleclass technology works, or how to work in collaboration with a workshop co-leader. You may want to add another healing modality to your toolkit in order to fully provide this package.

You don't have to keep changing your business cards as you add new talents. Your toolkit just gets stronger and more effective.

Stage 3 – Resonant pricing

Okay, *now* it's time to talk about pricing. Don't be tempted to let it interfere with earlier stages of this process. If you've been censoring your intuition, knocking off aspects to create a cheaper package, you will miss the solution your Tribe needs and people will be less likely to say yes to your service.

Comparison is of the devil

> *How have you priced before?*
>
> *How do you think you should price?*

Here's a conversation I had with Julie, the Brighton-based coach:

Julie: I've priced by comparing with how people price their massages. I know other coaches charge more – I paid £60 an hour with one woman but she has twenty years of experience so I need to charge less, right? [Pause] It feels fine.

Me: When you say "it feels fine", what do you mean?

Julie: [longer pause] Actually it doesn't feel fine. Now that I look at it, it feels really uncomfortable. It's like I look out and think: "I must make myself smaller, therefore cheaper, than her."

This conversation models how messy it can get when you price by comparison. You get into icky "I'm better, I'm worse" internal conversations. When you say to yourself, "Is my service as good as hers?" or "He trained for longer but my course was more rigorous" it becomes a minefield.

I want you to price in a way that has nothing to do with your self-esteem. I don't want you to price from your ego, from fear, or by looking at your so-called competition. We're going into a completely different territory for pricing.

The price is right

When it's time to plan your pricing, go to Connection. You'll find that the details are available when you start asking the right questions.

Resonant pricing transformed my business. I learned it from Mark Silver and Jason Stein at Heart of Business and it was a huge relief to discover I could price this way, rather than from my fearful ego. I've been able to raise my prices throughout the years and more and more people have said yes because they've been offered the right price.

Do you remember the '80s TV game show *The Price Is Right*? Contestants had to guess the price of certain desirable objects and if they guessed closest, they'd win them.

This is what resonant pricing feels like to me. It's as if there's a price that's already there for your package, and you just have to tune in to find out what it is. It's a simple and refreshing approach. Rather than getting your calculator out, looking at market rates and doing exhaustive analysis, you can tune in to your intuitive sense of the right price, the number that resonates like a tuning fork vibrating at the perfect pitch.

Resonant pricing exercise

As you think about your package, what is the lowest amount someone could pay you, below which you wouldn't be interested? Write that number down as the lowest in your range.

Now think about the highest amount someone could pay you for this service before you'd freak out and think they were being ridiculous. Write that number down as the highest number in your range.

You now have a range of numbers. You can do this next part by yourself but it helps to have someone talk you through. You could engage anyone for this – a friend, partner or even your child. All they're going to do is read up the range, starting with your lowest number and ending with your highest. (For example, if your range is from £20 to £200, they'd read "£20... £25... £30" and so on, at intervals up to £200.)

It would be a bonus if the person reading the numbers could share what *they* notice intuitively. If someone like that isn't easy to arrange, though, simply engage anyone who can read numbers out loud!

Once you've got your range (and ideally a "range reader"), bring your package back to mind. Often, people try to price their services before they're clear on what they're selling. Focus on the details of your package, the kind of person who's in your Tribe and which needs of theirs it serves, and why your package is an appropriate solution.

Bring to mind the lowest number in your range or get your reader to say it out loud for you. Then make your way up the range, noticing for each number what your intuition is telling you. Does your system feel good? Does it feel off or disconnected? You might feel an opening or closing, a warmth or coolness, a closeness or distance, or a "yes" or a "no" with each number.

Stay in your intuition as you consider each number, rather than trying to relate it back to market rates or what you hope or fear people can afford. You can do that later; for now, allow yourself to receive the information your system wants to give you. Prepare to be surprised!

Once you've completed this exercise, make a note of the number(s) that resonated. Don't censor yourself; just write down what you got. You will make sense of the numbers soon – don't stunt the process.

If you did the exercise with a reader, compare your resonant numbers with theirs.

Higher than expected?

It's normal for your resonant price to come back higher than you'd have imagined. It's also normal to freak out about this!

An artist was once asked to create a portrait for a customer. He took a mere ten minutes to paint a beautiful picture that the customer was delighted with, and the artist charged £5,000.

"£5,000 for ten minutes' work?" scoffed an onlooker

"No," replied the brilliant artist with a smile. "£5,000 for a lifetime's work."

This is one reason to price your services as a solution, rather than on an hour-by-hour basis. People aren't paying for your time. They're paying for everything it's taken you to get here, and for the transformation, the relief or the other benefits they're going to experience as a result.

Bottom line: we can't calculate the worth of what you offer in hours and minutes of visible work.

Onlookers may say you're too expensive or too cheap. This is true of virtually any product or service that exists. You can never price in a way that makes everyone happy! So, rest on your resonant price and trust that your right price will be the right fit for your right people.

This is another reason to research your Tribe's relationship with money. Does an outfit typically cost them £10, £100 or £1,000? What's normal for one Tribe won't make sense to another. The only people who are startled by my rates are those who aren't my Tribe. Someone in my Tribe simply responds, "Sounds great, how do I pay?"

Jacqueline, the coach who helps women with body anxiety, reported:

> *I was surprised that I felt nothing at the lower numbers in the range and I relaxed at the higher ones. I guess if I were a prospective client who had been dragging this issue around for years, I'd actually want to pay a lot of money, like that would signify I was committing and taking this seriously.*

Heart-led entrepreneurs tend to under-earn

Think about how much you'd be earning as an annual salary if you were in employment. There's no reason that following your passion independently should result in earning less than this, unless self-sabotage gets in the way. The pricing aspect of your business can be soul-nourishing. It's a chance for you to recognize your inherent worthiness, and receive. Trust that your heart knows what you can receive financially.

Do you shrink away from money matters or quickly discount your services? Faye, a piano teacher, recalled saying to a prospective client, "It's £25 per class. Is that all right?" She realized the question mark in her voice was giving her power away and resolved to address this.

Remember: a person in need is vulnerable. When you waver on your price, you remove a crucial degree of safety and this gives them an excuse to run away. You can help them trust they're taking a safe path by standing solid in your price.

Have you ever scared off a potential client – not because of the price but because of how you've communicated the price?

Have you been on the other side and lost confidence because someone sounded unclear about their price?

Lower than expected?

Sometimes it's a relief to find yourself resonating with a lower number. Other times, it can feel disappointing – and even scary.

Try it out. See how things go with charging a lower amount than you'd have liked, then repeat this exercise in a few months and notice what your intuition offers you then. As you lean in to your daily Connection practice and grow in your capacity to contribute and to receive, you're likely to find your heart can hold more.

More than one number?

It's normal to get two or three numbers that resonate. Depending on the nature of your package, one might be the early bird price and the other, the full price. Perhaps one number is what you can charge now and the other is what you can charge in a few years when you've added extra tools to your repertoire, or grown in confidence. Perhaps one number represents a concession, seasonal special or friends' rate.

Play lightly with these numbers, asking your intuition what each number is for. You'll soon realize you can get a feel for pricing, rather than needing to do laborious comparisons.

You're not responsible

You may have noticed that you were comfortable with the numbers when you did the resonant pricing exercise, whereas normally you aren't comfortable talking about money. One of the great assets of resonant pricing is that you're not responsible – in the nicest possible way. You're simply tuning in to what's right.

You know the expression, "great minds think alike"? Let's imagine there's one great mind: a collective unconscious. It makes sense that when a number clicks for you, it clicks for your prospective clients. It becomes irrelevant whether you're cheaper or more expensive than the so-called competition. Quite simply, people are more likely to say yes to your package if it is at a resonant price.

Once you've chosen a price that's right for you, you'll be more confident when telling people how much your services cost. If you're constantly doing market rate analysis and painstakingly trying to find where you fit in that range, you'll become anxious and hesitant. It's disorienting to try and orient yourself by what others are doing, rather than finding what's right for you.

You're unique. No-one else can provide the service you can, in the same way. How can you compare apples with pears?

No more stumbling

Intuitive packaging and resonant pricing are inherently reassuring. They help you find your unique position in the marketplace and make it easier to tell a prospective client how they can work with you and how much they are being asked to invest.

The sales process is sensitive, full of so many opportunities for the prospective client to back away. They need to feel safe enough to take those next steps with you. If you're stumbling over the details or the price, your prospective client will lose confidence in you; they'll have doubts and start back-tracking.

Once you have a resonant level of knowing, you can stand behind what you do, even if it's different from the industry standard.

> *How would it feel, to be unwavering on your price?*

An unusual way

I know this approach is different from what others might teach about how to make business decisions. All I can say is: it works. I feel safe when I lean in to this method of pricing. I know I'm consulting with the same intuitive mind that knows what I need financially.

This is where your business practices become synonymous with your Connection practices. You might have previously seen money as being disconnected from your spiritual path. Actually, the opposite can be true. Running a business and therefore having to set your prices gives you a reason to tune in to Source. You'll discover a refreshing sense of safety with this approach, and find you can trust that your needs will be met, as you focus on meeting the needs of others.

▶ Ready for action?

Firstly, intuitively package. Then, resonantly price.

Let's check in

Here's what you might have spotted in Step Four:

- **That you're not selling what you thought you were selling, but rather: solutions**

- **That the nuts and bolts of your offerings might come to you in a surprising way**

- **That trusting your intuition can be tricky but means you won't falter when asking for money**

Take a moment to gather up what you're taking from this step. Have you captured everything you want to? I invite you to reflect and make notes about your insights this far.

And let's check out

- **You know the importance of Connection**

- **You know the importance of defining and claiming your Tribe**

- **You know how to do heart-to-heart research**

- **You know how to package your passion and stand confidently behind your price**

It's now time to answer the question: how can you communicate with your Tribe about this perfect solution to their needs?

Let's move on to explore how to let people know you exist and that you can help them.

Step Five
Message

Step Five – Message

This step will enable you to:

- **Discover the inherent generosity of good marketing**

- **Enjoy the structure of a five-stage process for communicating with your Tribe**

- **Move away from staring at a blank screen or feeling tongue-tied**

Now you know what you're offering, it's time to communicate that to the people you help. Aside from the actual work you do, your core business activity is to create bonds with your Tribe. This communication has two halves.

The first half is your marketing message, which is the story you tell about your services. The second half relates to your marketing methods, which are the vehicles you choose to get that message across.

> *Before we dive in, take a moment to consider:*
>
> *What's your current relationship with marketing?*
>
> *What does the M word do to you?*

More resistance?

Have you noticed how much resistance there can be along this journey? Resistance to daily Connection, resistance to defining a niche, resistance to doing research, resistance to allowing your intuition to guide your package and price. And now you may encounter resistance to marketing.

Again, resistance isn't bad. In fact, it's usually protective. You're not being asked to throw away your discernment or questions. I want you to test each concept I offer; take it and see if it moves you into greater empowerment and success.

You might also find yourself thinking, "I should be sweeping away all these blocks right now. What was I waiting for?" I want to reassure you that taking time is okay. Sitting with the obstacles is okay. You will get there.

And while we're pausing, check how connected you're feeling. Has the voice of fear crept in? Or are you finding an unconditional sense of safety that allows you to engage with this material joyfully and without being overwhelmed?

Now is a great time to affirm the importance of Connection as the foundation of your daily activities. If you skipped your practice today, do it now and then return to these words and notice the difference.

Okay, back to marketing. Here are a few ways *Turn Your Passion To Profit* group participants have described their initial feelings about the M word:

> *It sounds crass, like someone is trying to get you to do something that isn't good for you but is good for them.*
>
> *It's about manipulating people into giving you money.*
>
> *I have a big wall, it's a dark art, there's no way into it.*
>
> *It sounds like something I can't do.*
>
> *It fills me with dread. It's overwhelming and I just want to hide.*

Ready to be surprised?

If this sounds like you, I want to say: thank you.

Seriously, thank you for recognizing that a huge amount of marketing out there *is* manipulative. Thank you for not buying into the myth that you need the next bigger, better, all-improved widget. Thank you for being discerning, for looking to your own needs rather than being swayed by million-pound marketing budgets.

Thank goodness for people like you. We need to stay awake and not buy in to whatever corporate marketeers decide is good for us. Your concerns about marketing are valid, and moreover, utterly necessary. You're primarily a citizen, not a consumer.

What breaks my heart is when you take your justified distaste for that kind of marketing and translate it into "I can't market these services that will actually help people." Then you add a whole bunch of other messy stuff to the mix – doubts about your self-worth, fear of being visible, fear of failure – and you're left with a heavy blanket of revulsion towards marketing, full stop.

This suffocates you and prevents you from communicating about your precious talents and passion. It will keep you stuck right where you are, unable to help the people who need you, unable to enjoy the impact or income you yearn for.

An unexpected love affair

I found that I loved marketing when it was framed in a different way – when I saw that it could be about connecting, helping and telling stories.

I realized that marketing could be generous: that *to market is to serve.* By embracing marketing, you can double the impact of your work. Sounds implausible? I trust that by the end of this step, you'll see how.

Good marketing is fundamentally about telling a good story. We love stories about heroes and their challenges, and this is the story you'll be telling in your business. You'll tell the story of your Love, Love, Money Tribe so that they can see themselves in it. People love – and need – to be seen and have their stories told back to them. You will do this as you market what you're passionate about.

Listen and tell

Developing a strong marketing message begins with listening to your Tribe. What are the patterns and the intricacies you see in the journeys of your research participants and existing clients? Once you've heard these, you'll know how to tell their story back to them. Then, when your Tribe encounter your marketing message, they will feel understood – like they're meant to hear this story.

Recently, I wanted to find a great parenting coach to recommend to a friend who was struggling with bringing up two children under five. A couple of coaches in the *Turn Your Passion To Profit* community came to mind, one of whom was Lorraine Burwood (who I mentioned in Step Three). I visited her website and was hooked immediately. The first line on her home page read, "Feeling a failure because raising your children is a constant battle?" and it went on to describe my friend's situation as if Lorraine knew her inside out. With a sigh of relief, I emailed Lorraine's link to my friend, reassured that here was a professional who could understand and empathize with what my friend was going through.

Lorraine had followed the step-by-step approach you're learning. She'd heard her Tribe's needs, in their own language, and was able to craft her marketing message so that it spoke powerfully and directly to anyone in that Tribe, as well as to anyone who knew someone who was.

You'll now learn how to create this kind of message to promote your services.

Every story fits within a genre and has certain narrative features

When your work is about helping, healing and serving, the story you'll be telling is the "solution-to-pain story".

With Step Three, you're capturing clear Before pictures. With Step Four, you're packaging and pricing your service as a solution, which will take people to longed-for After pictures – that is, where your Tribe will be once they've been helped by you.

This solution-to-pain genre, with its Before and After pictures, involves telling stories in a particular narrative order, which leads you to then position your service as the solution that makes sense, as the natural conclusion to your Tribe's story.

A story in five acts

There are five stages of the marketing message in this solution-to-pain genre. Once you've gained clarity on these five stages, you can use this message in both spoken interactions – for example, at networking events or when meeting new people – and in written form – for example, on a webpage or flyer.

Each stage covers one aspect of the story and there's a subplot (a tone, a quality) that accompanies each stage. Over the course of your five-stage message, you'll therefore convey to the reader or listener five core qualities. These are: empathy, respect, relief, hope and reassurance. (Pretty cool for marketing, right?)

In written form, each stage might be a paragraph, or a few lines. When you're speaking to someone, you'd simply include these five elements in the course of your conversation.

I've adapted this five-stage approach from Mark Silver who refers to it as the "customer-focused story"; he in turn had developed this from Robert Middleton's "marketing syntax".

The central idea for all three of us – and, of course, others – is that a marketing message is a story that you craft in a certain order, so that it makes sense.

Ready for the first stage? (Excited, even?)

Stage 1 – Aware of the pain
Subplot: Empathy

One of the main purposes of your research is to find out how your Tribe are doing *before* you get to them.

When you do your actual work, you'll learn how your client is doing. They'll open up to you and share their challenges, without needing to censor themselves. If you have an initial consultation, you'll hear someone's pain before they become a paying client.

Guess what? You don't have to wait until someone is your client, or even until they're in the initial consultation, to show you hear their pain. You can, and should, do that in your marketing.

In the first stage, speak or write about the pain that people experience before they hire you; the pain they're in that could *lead* them to hire you.

> **From your research and your work with clients, what's it like for someone before they find you?**

This is one of the most crucial things to know in business and yet so many business owners miss this point. Their website blares, "Get this! Get fantastic results!" and completely misses the fact that their visitor is not in that place.

Your prospective client has a problem. (Remember, this is a key feature of a niche, that these are people who share characteristics and share a common *problem*.)

Your prospective client is in a place of pain or need. They need you to meet them there.

> **What is the pain your prospective client would continue to be in if you didn't come along?**

This is the pain they will stay in if your marketing doesn't reach them.

This is why I believe that good marketing is your *duty* when you have something to offer that helps people. It's completely different from marketing some plastic widget you know will fall apart, or pushing insurance onto someone you know doesn't need it. If you know your services will genuinely make a difference in someone's life, it is selfish not to market. It's selfish to withhold information and fail to communicate the match between your service and their needs. A yoga teacher I spoke with recently said she felt like she had jewels in her pocket and that it was her responsibility to share them.

Put your client in the chair

Imagine a person who says, "Help me! I'm in need" and another person who looks at them and replies, "Well, I've got this thing that could help you but I'm not going to tell you about it." That's basically what happens when you hold yourself back from marketing.

When you start crafting your marketing message, imagine one of your ideal clients sitting with you. Do it now. Put a chair in front of you. Picture them sitting there, exactly how they'd be before you've come along. Say hello: greet them by name.

Now tune in to their inner world. What it's like to be them, right now?

The questions that follow will help you tune in to this ideal client. Just as in the Package and Price exercises, you'll be using your knowledge of your Tribe and tuning in to your intuition.

Be prepared to uncover answers you might not expect. We're looking for repeated, overlapping answers because they mean you're getting to the core of what your Tribe's situation is really like.

Write your answers down, as if you were writing directly to your ideal client. Write as much as you want for each answer, letting your intuition speak through you.

Hearing the need

Q1. What's a major challenge for them? Write as if you're looking at them, e.g. "A major challenge for you is carving out space for yourself", or "You're devastated to find out you can't have children".

Q2. What's the hardest thing about their situation? e.g. "The more you do, the further you get from what you're craving", or "It's causing distance between you and your partner."

Q3. Within this context, what are some things they haven't told anyone about?

Q4. What do they wish someone would understand, without them needing to explain?

Q5. What is it about their current situation that sometimes wakes them in the night?

Q6. What is it about their current situation that evokes strong emotions in them – perhaps crying, rage or helplessness?

Q7. What would be the cost of staying in this situation for another year?

Q8. What would it be like for them if this never changed?

You'll recognize some of these questions from Step Three, of course. Your research responses will give you the exact words and feelings to include here.

How was it to answer?

Ruth, a voice coach, found that answering these questions was the breakthrough she needed to define her Tribe. She knew the people who were coming to her and it was easier to tune in to their inner world than to find a label for them.

You might notice how much you personally identify with your Tribe – like it's you sitting on that chair. This is normal – your true Tribe is often, as we explored in Step Two, made up of people going through what you once went through (or what you still struggle with at times).

You might also become aware of an emotional component. By the end of those eight questions, you're likely to have a strong sense of the pain this kind of person is in. That emotional aspect offers an even more compelling reason to market your service.

Connect with the pain

That pain of your Tribe makes it your *duty to market.* On a bad day, when you're feeling disconnected from the meaning of it all, it's what reminds you that people need you and that you need to make sure they can find you.

Your prospective clients are going about the world in that pain. For the most part, their pain is invisible to the people around them. They're feeling frustrated, anxious, disempowered, stuck, uncomfortable, dissatisfied, confused, isolated or unfulfilled, but most marketing doesn't reach this depth. It skims the surface.

One of the participants in *Turn Your Passion To Profit* said:

> *As I went through those questions, I felt like screaming out: "Nooooo, you can't stay like this for another year!" It was powerful.*

Starting to write her marketing message reminded her why she does what she does. People in a particular situation need her, and they need to know she's here and that she has intentionally set herself up to support them.

Feel it in your bones

I want you to have that same kind of feeling, that feisty determination, that it's not okay for your Tribe to feel like this, not on your watch. Not when you know you have something that can help.

I spent a few months in my early twenties doing street fundraising for a charity that helps the homeless. It was winter, London was cold and it wasn't fun standing around all day asking passers-by for money. But as I felt that chill in my bones, I found renewed energy. I knew that the people I was raising funds for didn't have the luxury of going back home and warming up. That cold represented why I was asking people to donate and is what spurred me on.

Remember Amanda, the intuitive logo designer? Her goal is to create "life logos" that help entrepreneurs focus on their deepest purpose. Her initial perspective was that no-one would go looking for that but rather would stumble upon it accidentally. She hadn't connected her idea with the concept of a person's need. After doing this exercise, she saw that what she's offering could be a solution to a challenge her Tribe do know they have. She moved from wondering, "Who'd need a life logo?" to seeing the deeper hunger it would meet. She felt more confident and reassured about why she was being called so strongly in that direction.

Guidelines for Stage 1

Describe your prospective client's problem/situation, writing to them in the second person: "You are..."

Use their words. These might come to you intuitively; perhaps you've heard a repeated phrase in your research. Often, your Tribe will use specific language or a particular metaphor, for example, "me time", "juggling", "drowning", "hitting a wall", "struggling", or "craving headspace".

Linda Anderson, an Emotional Freedom Technique practitioner, knows that unconscious blocks keep her clients from embracing the sales and marketing activities they need to engage in to build their business. However, they wouldn't have that awareness or use that language themselves. From their perspective, it feels like there's "an invisible wall" between them and their prospective clients.

They might say, "No matter what I do, I can't seem to get to them." It makes more sense, and is more engaging, to present the situation from your Tribe's point of view.

Highlight the most painful aspects. I know this can be hard – you want to avoid discomfort – but it's important that you don't censor your understanding. You're not manipulating their pain. The pain is there. Your duty is to hear it and communicate that you recognize it and can ease it.

If your prospective client doesn't spot that you "get" where they're at, it'll be harder for them to reach out and communicate with you. So show them that you understand, and your empathy will powerfully engage them.

Stage 2 – The hard work so far
Subplot: Respect

In this stage, you acknowledge and articulate what your prospective client may have already tried in their efforts to alleviate their situation.

Perhaps they've read books or visited websites. Perhaps they've worked with other practitioners who use different techniques. Perhaps they've already changed some habits or aspects of their lifestyle.

You may hear some of these in your initial consultations, and you definitely want to ask about this in your research.

> *What else has your Tribe turned to?*
>
> *Who else is set up to meet this kind of need?*

In this stage, you're reminded that this is not a two person game, involving just you and your prospective client. You both exist in a much wider context of services and products.

Your prospective client is the hero of this story. Their previous attempts might have stalled or failed but they're still the hero. Convey that you know they're intelligent and committed to improving or resolving their situation. You're empathizing with their frustration that previous solutions haven't (completely) worked out.

Let's take the example of Joy, the osteopath. When a new client comes to her for help with Repetitive Strain Injury (RSI), he's likely to have visited his GP, been offered painkillers, and gone on the waiting list for physiotherapy. Frustrated by the wait, perhaps he's gone on the internet and found a few exercises to try. Maybe he also found a book in the library and has been trying to implement those suggestions. His friend, who also had RSI, has given him advice but now he's starting to feel confused by all the different strategies.

When Joy reaches the second paragraph of her marketing message, she would put all this in writing, starting, "You've been to the GP but you're not so happy about taking painkillers indefinitely", and so on.

Becca Harrison is passionate about make-up as a tool for women to feel more confident and empowered. She offers one-to-one "Aphrodite sessions" and workshops. Her paragraph would start, "You've pulled pages from magazines with eye make-up tutorials and then put them in a file you've never looked at again. You've gone to the department store make-up counter and got exasperated" – and so on.

Saluting the hero

When you realize how much your prospective clients have been trying, you can fill this second paragraph with deep acknowledgement and respect. It's likely that your prospective client will feel frustrated or even like a failure. They'll be thinking, "I can't try anything else, I've already thrown money down the drain, is this never going to go away?"

Communicate that you know they've been trying. Acknowledge them as resourceful.

What if they haven't?

What if you're the first port of call? What if someone hasn't tried anything else?

Although they might not have reached out to another professional, it's likely they'll have bemoaned the situation with a friend or partner, or at least done a general internet search. Even if they've just been thinking about this issue, going round and round in their mind about it – that's doing something. You can even say, "You've been hoping this problem would go away of its own accord."

If they haven't recognized and started considering their situation, they're unlikely to be on your website, reading your marketing message. Remember: your Tribe know they have a challenge and are prepared to take action and spend money in order to resolve it.

So, when it comes to this section, mention the common strategies your prospective clients might have been trying and imbue your words with acknowledgement and respect.

Stage 3 – Why other attempts haven't worked
Subplot: Relief

This stage is about why other attempts haven't fully worked.

It's time to give your prospective client a lightbulb moment. Reassure them that they are not stupid, lazy or destined to fail in resolving this challenge.

There are reasons why they haven't had (full) success when applying the other strategies. Certain key elements were missing – and you're going to show them what those elements are.

Here's how my version might start:

Most marketing advice doesn't work for people like you because it's not congruent with your values, your ethics, and doesn't relate to purpose-led and passion-led businesses. It's also aimed at small to medium companies and you're just one person, doing it all.

The reader feels relief; the penny drops. "Ah so that's why I haven't 'got' marketing before. It's not me! It's the strategies I was choosing."

Nina is a coach whose Tribe are mothers returning to paid work. In the previous stage (2), she writes:

You've flicked through women's magazines and seen various career articles. You've been chatting with other mums at the school gates. Once the kids are in bed, you lie there with ideas going round and round, and now and again get up for midnight forum searches on MumsNet.

In Stage 3, she writes:

But you're alone with your thoughts, or you're consulting people who aren't experts. With all of this, there's no partnership. As supportive as your friends may be, they don't know the right questions to ask you to move you forward and they also have their own agendas.

Have a rant

As you write this paragraph, let it flow as if you were writing an email directly to your Tribe. Be impassioned! You care that these solutions haven't quite hit the spot – after all, that's why you're doing what you're doing, with your unique slant. Be on your Tribe's side; take a stand on their behalf.

An interior designer might say:

I know you've been looking in beautiful magazines but those designs aren't specific to you, they don't take into account your lifestyle – and also they're two-dimensional!

With them

You are totally on your Tribe's side throughout. You are acknowledging, understanding, empathizing, respecting. You are not saying, "Ah poor you, look at these stupid options you've chosen, no wonder you're not getting anywhere. Let me sweep in with my expertise and put you out of your misery." That's not what this is about.

Think about when you've been a client. It's embarrassing to try and to fail. It can make you anxious, wary about spending another penny on bad choices. It's a relief when a new practitioner explains what was missing; it helps you feel less foolish about your past lack of success.

Once again, this is not about you bad-mouthing the competition. Don't make anyone else look wrong in this stage – or indeed, ever! Simply offer understanding and explanation. Empathize and educate, don't judge or manipulate.

Save them

You want to help your Tribe with their challenges so they save time and money. It's a radically alternative view of marketing, which is so often perceived as inciting people to waste money! You don't want your people to waste any more effort wandering down fruitless paths.

> *What elements might have been missing in previous attempts your Tribe have made?*

Some possibilities:

- **No accountability**
- **Not frequent enough**
- **Didn't go deep enough**
- **It needed to be more experiential**
- **It needed to be more physical, less cerebral**
- **It needed to be more practical, less theoretical**
- **It was an off-the-shelf solution, not specific to their situation**
- **There was no partnership**
- **There was no professional expertise**
- **There was no heart-to-heart understanding**

Stage 4 – The way forward
Subplot: Hope

You've listed what they've tried and why that hasn't (fully) worked. This next stage is the natural follow-up, where you outline what they need instead.

Emphasize what you know works about your approach: its unique and particularly effective characteristics. This will naturally correlate with what hasn't worked for your Tribe before.

If they've felt alone and isolated, for example, then what they need is to have someone on their side every step of the way. If previous solutions have been overly intellectual, then what's called for is transformational work that involves physicality.

Your approach, but not you

You may have noticed you're not in the picture yet. Throughout your marketing message, your role is as a helpful, empathetic information source. You serve by showing you understand.

In Stage 4, you give a prescription for what is needed but you're not saying they have to get it from you. Why? Because they don't. Even if you stopped doing your thing, you'd want someone else to do it, because it works.

If Nina, the coach working with mothers, stopped working with her Tribe, she'd still be saying to her friend at the playground, "You need someone on your side, who has expertise, who can partner with you."

Stay invisible

Right up to the end of the marketing message, you're invisible. You're authentically helping someone understand their current situation and what they need. It's about them, not you.

You're an information provider, an educator, an expert in this particular situation who can advise them, from your heart.

> *What do you genuinely believe this person needs that is different from what they've tried before?*
>
> *What do they need that they might not have found so far?*

Some possibilities:

- **To meet in the comfort of their own home**
- **Group support**
- **An energetic healing element**
- **In-person connection**
- **The convenience of phone appointments**
- **More frequent sessions**
- **More physical/experiential sessions**

Start this paragraph with, "What you need instead is..." or "Imagine..."

Here's the magic

One of the reasons I fell in love with marketing is that it's an opportunity to serve. In Stage 4, you are giving your Tribe a prescription of love. "If I could wave a magic wand for you and your situation, you'd have a practitioner who comes to your house with massage oil, music and candles in hand." Or, "If I could wave a magic wand, you'd have a remedy that takes your whole life into account", or "you'd share this journey with like-minded buddies".

Remember, Stage 3 was about the lightbulb moment. But if you left your Tribe there, they'd still have a degree of frustration. "Great! I get it! But it's still not working."

Stage 4 is about hope. There may be a way out of frustration, ill health, stuckness, loneliness or relationship challenges. "This is what life is like for you now, this is what you've tried, this is why that hasn't (fully) worked, and so here's what you can have instead."

Margaret Hiley, who offers the German-to-English translation services for academics, might write:

You've been seeking linguistic help from a general translator who's not an expert in your academic field. Imagine instead that you were to work with an academic translator, in close collaboration, liaising with them at every stage of the translation. You'd feel involved in the process and you'd be confident that your work was being understood the way you want it to be.

Your unique qualities as a professional will come through here – for example, Margaret's passion for empowerment and collaboration.

Forget marketing speak

Think of your marketing message as story-telling. Bear in mind that you're offering something people really need, rather than trying to find what sets you apart from "the competition". Simply tell the story that you see, as someone who knows your Tribe inside out.

If the mums are content to talk with their friends about career plans, great. They're not Nina's Tribe. If the office worker with RSI is getting on fine with their doctor and physio, great. They don't need Joy and her osteopathy.

Your Tribe are those people who aren't fine, who do need you and your unique form of support.

Don't try to use marketing language or censor your natural expression because you think that's what's expected when crafting website copy. When you write like you would speak, your Tribe will hear it with their hearts. They'll see themselves in your mirror.

In this paragraph, check that you're explaining:

- **What would work instead**

- **The strategies or approach you advocate (remembering that it's not yet about your services specifically)**

- **What makes this different from previously attempted solutions**

- **How their situation would be improved with this solution in place (for example, "you'll feel supported" or "you'll feel in collaboration")**

By the end of Stage 4, the member of your Tribe reading or hearing your message will likely feel a real sense of hopefulness. Then, a yearning sets in which leads us to:

Stage 5 – The perfect match
Subplot: Reassurance

Up until now, it's not been about you. It's not been about Shamanic healing or nutrition or craniosacral therapy. It's been about them.

You have remained invisible in the marketing. You've been an anonymous voice of helpfulness, focusing on the person who's in front of you, reading or hearing the message, and what they need.

In this final stage, it's time for you to appear.

Not so fast

You are not, however, racing onto the stage to a great fanfare, taking a bow. It's much more matter-of-fact. Almost an afterthought.

Gently and naturally make the connection between their need and why you're the perfect person to offer the service you've been advocating (your approach, experience, and background).

Include any relevant qualifications. Who did you train with? For how long? What certificates do you hold? What evidence do you have of the effectiveness of your tools and approach?

Think about what *you* would need to know if you were the prospective client, sitting in that imaginary chair.

> *What would reassure you about the integrity and competence of a practitioner?*

Get these down on paper and be proud. And, as useful as credentials are, there's a whole other piece to Stage 5.

"Put your mess in your message"

I heard this from Suzanne Evans, a fellow marketing coach. Yes, you want to come across as reliable, qualified and professional. However, it can be just as reassuring for your Tribe to know that you've struggled with something similar to them. It adds a level of solidarity – that you're a soul sister, not a judgmental holier-than-thou expert on a pedestal.

You made space for their pain; don't censor yours. Reveal the particular essence of your life story that is relevant to show why you're brilliantly placed to help them with their need.

Chloe is a slender, toned, statuesque personal trainer. You might be in dire need of support with your fitness goals but might hold back from hiring her, thinking, "Ah, she's so beautiful and has it all together." You might fear she wouldn't understand how stuck you're feeling with this aspect of life.

However, imagine if Chloe shared that, for a long time, she avoided looking in the mirror because she didn't like what was looking back at her. She felt at war with her body, dreaded clothes shopping, and got out of breath just walking up a few flights of stairs.

Hearing or reading that, you'd realize, "Wow, maybe we're not so dissimilar after all" and feel safe enough to reach out.

One of your greatest assets

Kris Carr and Polly Noble both teach healthy nutrition and lifestyle habits because they were diagnosed with cancer and decided to find out what would keep them alive.

> *When you were in need, what helped you?*
>
> *Did you learn how to do marketing because you were struggling financially? (Me!)*
>
> *Did the Lightning Process help cure your chronic fatigue?*
>
> *Did coaching help you find the courage to leave an unhappy marriage?*
>
> *Did yoga help you lose weight?*
>
> *Did acupuncture help you get pregnant?*

Include your own Before and After pictures in your marketing message, describing your situation with words and (if appropriate) photos if there is visible evidence of your transformation. I've seen raw food coaches display old photographs where they look overweight, pasty and acne-ridden and then of them metamorphosed into slender beings with glowing skin. Those pictures are compelling and show that these people are walking their talk.

Joy explained why she loves helping people who have RSI. This would be her final paragraph, after she'd empathized with the problem, listed the existing solutions, and offered some education:

> *The reason I know all of this is that I had RSI myself. I had two hands that didn't work for half a year. I know what it's like to not be able to chop vegetables. It was a hard experience – and I've come out the other end. I can literally wave my two hands at you and show that this doesn't have to last forever.*

Feel free to paint a picture and give details in this stage, like Joy did with the example of chopping vegetables. Describe that pivotal moment where you shouted at your child and heard yourself sounding like the mother you vowed you'd never become, which is how you found your way to Nonviolent Communication, or parent coaching. Describe that painful argument with your colleague when you realized enough was enough and decided that meditation would help you find more inner calm. Or what it was like to lose a best friend to suicide, which is what catalysed you to train as a psychotherapist.

Don't pretend you're flawless

Your Tribe want you to be human and accessible. They will trust you if they know you've been there, you've walked through territory they can identify with.

You're still an expert and you can be relied upon, but your humanity makes you more believable and authentic. You become credible not just because of the training you've done, but because of who you are and what you've lived through.

When you write this paragraph, connect with the personal experience that brought you into this field. Share the essence of your story and include pictures, both figuratively and literally.

In summary, Stage 5 is where you:

- **Explain why you're the perfect person to help**
- **Offer a balance of:**

   (1) Your professional credibility: your training, qualifications, previous client success stories

   (2) Your unique life experience, personality and the characteristics of your service

Your Tribe care most about the second element but like to be reassured by the first, so include both.

After reading or hearing this part, your Tribe should totally get why you're the perfect person to be offering this service.

▶ Ready for action?

Get your pen and paper or computer ready, imagine your ideal client sitting on the chair opposite you, and write them a short paragraph for each stage, using your natural voice and making sure your heart and empathy are switched on.

This is your basic, bare-bones promotional copy. Read it back. Can you see why someone would want to work with you? This is what happens when you position your service as the natural conclusion to a story of struggle. This is the impact of creating a business that is needs-based and all about solutions.

Use your five-stage marketing message wisely – it has real impact. It's a way of giving your Tribe (1) empathy, (2) respect, (3) relief, (4) hope, and (5) reassurance, without asking anything in return.

The price of a solution

After your basic five-step marketing message, now is the time to explain the logistics of your service, the details you came up with in the last step. How many, how much, where and how.

The question of price, as we looked at in the previous step, becomes somewhat irrelevant. Whether your service costs £20, £200 or £2,000, it makes sense to your Tribe when they compare it against the cost of staying where they are, trying solutions that don't work.

In addition to the logistics, you could also include testimonials you've already gathered and answers to frequently asked questions.

What's missing?

There's one core element missing from this marketing message now: your call to action.

As you've read your story back, hopefully you can hear that the natural conclusion is "... and they worked together happily ever after." That is your story's ending – or rather, the beginning.

Put that final stepping stone down for your Tribe. Give them the relief of crossing over from water onto solid ground with a call to action.

You're doing this from a place of service, rather than manipulation. This person is in need, they're yearning to learn more about this solution that will help, so be kind and tell them exactly what they need to do next.

> ### *What is your specific next step?*

Some possibilities:

- "Click here to get started"
- "Phone me within office hours (9am – 5pm) or leave a voicemail at other times"
- "Fill out this web form"
- "Click the yellow PayPal button below"
- "Write your name and email address on this list"

Make it super-easy

Don't be afraid to spell out the call to action. This is not because your prospective client is stupid but because they're busy. There should be no question in their mind about what to do next.

We'll look more at the Flow from stranger to paying client in Step Seven, but for now, recognize that with high-end services (like an ongoing programme or an intensive residential course), you're unlikely to invite the prospective client to buy straight away. There will be an interim step, such as a free consultation. Direct them to that.

By the end of Stage 5, those people who are genuinely your Tribe are likely to be internally saying, "Yes". By giving them a tangible action step, you give them the chance to express that "Yes". Make sure the action is immediate, so they can say "Yes" now.

Many self-employed people miss out the call to action. They resist, thinking, "If she really wants help, she'll get in touch some way."

Be much more generous than that. Make this step clear, easy, specific and immediately actionable.

How are you feeling?

That's a lot of information. You've got a lot to work with, so how are you doing?

You might have increased clarity. Great. You might also feel overwhelmed or confused. These are uncomfortable yet common companions on the path of self-employment.

If you find you don't know what to include in each of these five stages, it's time to go back to research. Step Five reminds you why it's so important to hear your Tribe speak in their own voices, explaining their situation. Getting in touch with their needs is likely to give you the fire to get on with it. You'll realize that these people are waiting to hear your marketing message.

Your cloak of invisibility

As you look back over your marketing message, check that you're mostly invisible and that it's need-focused and Tribe-focused.

Imagine you're looking for a holiday. A friend of yours recommends a hotel so you search online to find out more about the hotel. Right?

Not quite. You go to the website to find out about you. You look at that site wondering: how comfy is that bed for *me*? How far is it from the station in terms of how I need to organize *my* travel?

Make sure your message works as a mirror. Make sure it's directed at your Tribe, it speaks to them and answers their questions. Then, they'll be able to see themselves.

Let's check in

Here's what you might have spotted in Step Five:

- **That marketing is a service, it's generous, and to hold back is selfish**

- **That the natural flow of a marketing story is easy to write and talk with people about**

- **That you're not going to bore your Tribe with *you*, but stun them with how well you know *them***

Take a moment to gather up what you're taking from this step. Have you captured everything you want to? I invite you to reflect and make notes about your insights this far.

And let's check out

- **You know the importance of Connection**

- **You know the importance of defining and claiming your Tribe**

- **You know how to do heart-to-heart research**

- **You know how to package your passion and stand confidently behind your price**

- **You know the message you want to communicate**

It's now time to answer the question: how does that message reach your Tribe?

Let's move on to explore ways you can reach those people who need you.

Step Six
Methods

Step Six – Methods

This step will enable you to:

- **Choose communication vehicles that most effectively get your message to your Tribe**

- **Explore a plethora of marketing methods and assess which suit you and your Tribe**

- **Discover out-of-the-box ways to communicate**

In this step, we're getting into the nuts and bolts of marketing so ensure you're connected before you proceed. It'll make the difference between skimming and getting overwhelmed versus going at a healthy pace, engaged and alert.

Your message needs legs and wings

You now have a basic marketing message. It's sitting there as a text document on your computer, or handwritten on a sheet of paper, which is exactly where it should start. It's now time to set your message free. It's time to get your message to your Tribe.

This is where we encounter the fundamental question: how do you get access to your Tribe?

I tricked you a little

In Step Three, I asked you to spread the word about your research using your preferred communication methods. That was a cheeky way of getting you to explore different marketing methods.

Make a note now of all the methods you used to find research participants. Now, circle those methods that were most effective.

You can use these same methods when it comes to communicating your solution-to-pain story. You also now have more information about where your Tribe hang out from asking that question in your research, and from trial and error.

Don't get it right

As with everything you're learning in this *Turn Your Passion To Profit* approach, throw away the compulsion to *get it right*. You might have already started worrying that you need to choose The Right Methods. Instead, see this as an experiment. Play with different communication options, discover which fit you best, and keep it all as simple and enjoyable as you'll allow it to be.

There's an abundant menu of marketing methods to choose from. Some will be a more obvious fit for who you are and who your Tribe are. As you read the examples, notice which feel intriguing (even if a bit daunting) and which turn you off.

Ready for the menu?

When someone is new to self-employment, they often think *business cards* are evidence that they've officially arrived. A business card is an easy way of giving your contact details to someone. Website, social media profile, phone number – these are ways of maintaining a link.

But if you're paying for business cards, let's super-charge them. That pocket-sized item can do a lot.

Here are some elements to include:

1 – A line that enables your Tribe to recognize themselves. For example: "Helping mothers enjoy a smooth return to work" or "Massage for over-worked tattoo artists".

2 – A call to action that tells someone exactly what to do with the card. For example: "For free articles, visit: *www.youinspireme.co.uk*" or "To book your free consultation, phone ....." Or you could include a question. I met a consultant who had printed on the back of her cards: "What does authentic leadership mean to you?" and she invited me to email my answer. I did – which got us into email contact. Give someone a reason to stay connected with you. Your card then has an active purpose, rather than a reason to be shoved away in a drawer and forgotten about.

3 – A photo of you. Your prospective clients are busy and meet lots of people; they may get home with your business card and wonder, "Now, which one was Sandra? Who was the woman who talked to me about Pilates?" A photo on your card associates you with the person they met at that event.

Do you like faces?

Nina likes people. She chats with her Tribe of mums at the school gates. She goes knocking on her neighbours' doors. She's well known by her local grocer and, when his customers tell him they're thinking about going back to work, he recommends Nina and directs them to the pile of her *flyers* he allows her to display.

Joy's work as an osteopath has a geographical focus so it makes sense for her to attend *networking events* and build strong *cross-referral links* with other local complementary therapists.

Online community?

Claire Bradford has made *Facebook* work for her. Her page is buzzing because she encourages interaction. She runs two weekly themes: Turbo Tuesday where she motivates participants to blast through their backlog and tackle their To Do list, and Throw Out Thursday where she asks people to post what they're letting go of to make their life lighter. She interacts with her Tribe, helps them, and showcases what it's like to have her energy on their side, spurring them on.

Madeleine Giddens has established an impressive *online presence*, with a *website, social media profiles* and a *newsletter* to share her love of herbs. Your newsletter could be a masterpiece in design, with your logo and pictures, or you could use a plain text format. You could deliver content in the body of your broadcast emails or refer people to your website.

For Margaret's work as a translator, it's important that she has international reach and so she attends academic *conferences* around the globe. She also emails her existing academic network. In the early days of business, activating your *existing email contact list* is a useful way of letting people know what you do.

The list goes on

As you read, which methods are you gravitating towards?

There is no one-size-fits-all prescription for this. Each method has its strengths and the one that works best for me or her won't necessarily be the best fit for you. Who knows, you might invent marketing methods that no-one has tried before!

Do you need a website?

A website can be phenomenally useful for your business – some would say, essential. Regardless of where you are or what you're doing, it represents you 24/7. Your Tribe can find you from anywhere in the world and can access information about you and your approach, on their own terms, in their own time. It's a safe way of engaging and if you learn a little about *search engine optimization* (how people can find you when they type words and phrases into search engines), then you can quickly be found by hundreds – even thousands – of potential clients.

I recommend WordPress, which builds your website around a blog page, gives you easy access to update content, creates a site that is quickly noticed by search engines, and offers hundreds of additional free and helpful (and easy-to-use) widgets and plug-ins to customize your online presence. You can choose from a variety of themes (design templates) to set the overall look and functionality of your site.

If you read those last two paragraphs and felt out of your depth, you're in good company. The prospect of creating a website has stopped many brilliant people in their tracks. It can feel like an almighty beast of a task, huge and overwhelming and out of your comfort zone.

I advocate getting help when tasks feel overwhelming. Here are a couple of affordable ways to do that:

1 – Hire a web developer to set up WordPress and hosting for your domain name (your web address). They can also help you choose and customize a theme and set up any widgets you might like. This was the route I took, with the fantastic support of Adam Kayce (see Links and Resources).This approach is typically less expensive than asking a web developer to create a website from scratch. Also, you'll end up with a site you can easily manage yourself, rather than having to keep deferring to a developer for changes and updates.

2 – Follow a step-by-step DIY guide. Check out Laura Roeder's free End Your Website Shame webinars (see Links and Resources). If you like her approach, you can opt for one of her paid-for Zero To WordPress home-study products. If you run into glitches, you can engage the help of a web-savvy friend or hire a web developer like Adam.

There are people out there who can handle technical glitches in a fraction of the time it would take you to figure out what's going on so lean in to that support. It's a worthwhile investment.

Not ready for a website?

If you're not yet at the point of wanting a full website, that doesn't mean you can't have an online presence. You could use blogging software, a Facebook Page, a YouTube channel or an EventBrite event. You could write up your marketing message as an article and post it to online article directories. If you aren't ready to pay for a domain name, web hosting and a web developer, there are free and low-cost options available.

Your online presence can act as a store for your marketing message (the five-stage message, plus the logistics and your call to action) and you can then do other activities to keep guiding people to that place.

Get found

You might spend a lot of time, money and effort putting up a website and then get frustrated when you don't get many hits. Ask yourself:

> *How would someone in your Tribe actually find your site?*

There are strategies for optimizing your site for search engines. If someone needs a massage in Cheltenham, they'd probably type "massage Cheltenham" into Google. If you'd like these people to find your site, optimize your website using keywords like these. My sister-in-law, Gemma Gordon, is an acupuncturist in Cambridge; search for "acupuncture Cambridge" and you're likely to find her at the top of the list.

Optimization is a complex concept but in a nutshell is about (1) knowing the kind of words your Tribe use when they search online for what they need, and (2) including those keywords in your content and also in the high-status parts of your website, like the domain name, page titles and blog post titles. If you opt for a WordPress website, you can add a plug-in and fill out the fields with your keywords.

Search engines like Google and Yahoo check to see that they give browsers links to websites that closely match what they're looking for. So, know what your Tribe is looking for – and be a close match!

In your research and with your existing clients, listen for words your Tribe use to describe their needs. As already noted, in your research, ask directly: What would you type into a search engine, to try and resolve your situation?

Gemma's ideal acupuncture clients might not realize they need acupuncture, so wouldn't search for that term, but might type in "alternative pain relief" or "drug-free headache cure" and be delighted to discover she exists.

This is another reason why it's critical to define your Tribe clearly. If you help "everyone", what are your keywords? On the other hand, if you coach about marriage difficulties, your keywords might be "relationship", "stuck", "marriage" and "unhappy". If your Tribe are menopausal women, your keywords might include "hot flushes" and "hormonal".

SEO sounds confusing?

Don't worry, search engine optimization is just one way of getting people to your website. I didn't get interested in this until I was several years into running You Inspire Me. It's something you can delegate but that would only be worth your money (and the other person's time) if you've got a clear picture of your Tribe and how they'd describe their needs.

There are other ways your Tribe can find your website, for example:

- **Add your website link to your email signature**

- **Be linked to and from other websites**

- **Post comments on related forums**

- **Register with online directories and local print directories**

- **Register on Google Maps**

- **Include your website link on your business cards**

- **Link to your site from your social media accounts**

How about networking?

I love meeting people, being in community and seeing our interdependence. It makes business life more fun, too.

There's the good old-fashioned, in-person way of networking where you attend official events or hang out at the places your Tribe tend to circulate.

Which events should you choose? As ever, refer back to your research and growing knowledge of your Tribe. Which events do your Tribe attend? If your Tribe aren't there, it's probably not a good use of your precious business time.

The two-hat trick

You might find that you're already part of a community where your Tribe hang out. This isn't essential, but can certainly be useful.

As a yoga teacher, you might attend the Yoga Show as a visitor and, as you browse the stalls or stand in the lunch queue, meet people who would love to come to your next workshop. If you're an adoptive parent who offers training and support to other adoptive parents, then you'll be wearing an extra hat when attending a national family conference. You're simultaneously a member of this Tribe *and* someone who supports this Tribe.

This can make networking easy. Leanne Callaby is a massage therapist who loves to work with tattoo artists and bikers. She fits in with this group because her husband has been a photographer for a leading tattoo magazine for over a decade and she's had several large tattoos drawn herself. It's no hardship for her to find and hang out with her Tribe.

Clodagh Beaty knows what it's like to start your own business as an ex-pat in Spain so she fits right in at her Tribe's hang-outs. You might catch her having a glass of Rioja at a networking event in Madrid, talking about how to reduce stress.

Where are you considered "one of them"?

When you go to a work event, wedding, Christmas party or collect your kids from school, you will naturally interact with people who might be your Tribe. Don't hold back – it's okay for people to know what you do.

Make a note now of a few places where you could physically meet your Tribe.

Top tips for successful networking

While it can be helpful to have business cards with you when you attend events, you don't need to make this complicated or burdensome. A simple card with your details, a one-liner about your Tribe, a call to action and possibly a photo can be ordered from a company like Vistaprint for a few pounds.

However, it's far more useful for you to walk away with *their* card (or details). When you go to a networking event, whether it's set up officially in that way, or it's simply a social occasion, wear your market research hat. You're not there to sell your wares and thrust your business card into someone's hand. I've met that kind of person (you probably have too) and it's a major turn off.

Instead, make it your mission to develop your knowledge of your Tribe. When you meet someone in your Tribe (or someone who knows your Tribe), be curious. Be the person everyone loves at parties – who's genuinely interested and listens and doesn't just talk about themselves all night.

It may be that in the natural flow of conversation, your marketing message comes through in spoken form. Great! For example, Joy meets Rob at her boyfriend's work event and Rob starts telling her about the pain in his arms and wrists; she listens, she's nodding, she's understanding – and Rob doesn't even know she's an osteopath, it's just a social conversation.

She has entered Stage 1 of her marketing message – space for the challenges to be heard.

Like any concerned listener, she might instinctively ask, "So what have you tried already?" Stage 2.

With a tone of dejection, Rob lists off a few things. Joy might reply with empathy, "Ah yeah, what I often find is missing in those approaches is..." Stage 3 – and so it continues.

That might read as formulaic but in real-life situations, it makes for flowing conversation. Remember: your marketing message is a story that makes narrative sense, so it is the kind of conversation you'd naturally have with a person in your Tribe.

In fact, you might find it's easier to communicate your message in spoken situations because you're interacting in real time and tailoring your responses to that one person. You can (and should) slant your basic message according to the unique situation of the person you're with.

Hate networking events?

Some people dread official networking events because they think they have to deliver a thirty second pitch to each new person they meet.

Focus instead on the five-step message. Go with the intention to listen and be curious, provide useful information about what might be missing and what might be needed, and then be ready to complete your message with who you are and why you got into this. Then give the person something to do – make your call to action.

For example, say, "If you want to find out more, the first step is a free consultation. I have slots on Tuesday and Thursday afternoon, by phone. Here's my email address, drop me a short email telling me which afternoon would suit you and I'll let you know what times I've still got available that day."

Even better, if you've got your diary with you, book their free consultation then and there. Why wait?

The sales bit

Do you find the call to action piece challenging because it feels like selling? Then simply ask if they'd be willing to be interviewed.

Remember Linda Anderson, the EFT practitioner who was one of the examples in Step Three? I originally met her at the Mind Body Spirit Festival in Cambridge. We got chatting and I asked if she'd be willing to help with my research. She was, so I made a note of her email address in my diary and wrote down her general availability. When I got home, I emailed her with a few possible times to talk. We did the interview, which was very helpful for me, and a few months later she booked on to my next *Turn Your Passion To Profit* group. If the first thing I'd said to her was, "Oh, hi, would you like to join my programme?" it wouldn't have made any sense.

Be compassionate and patient with yourself if you find this part difficult. Even if your call to action is to book a free consultation or research interview, you're still asking for a level of commitment from someone. It's normal to have worries about sales. Step Seven will show you how to take someone through from stranger, to interested potential client, to committed client.

Social networking

It's a funny term, but *social networking* refers to online networking using platforms such as Facebook, Twitter and LinkedIn.

If you decide to use these methods for marketing, firstly take a look at *your profile*. Use this space to sum up what you do and for whom. Your profile can be a mirror for your Tribe, confirmation that they've come to the right place.

For example, Tad Hargraves: "Tad teaches green, local, independent, holistic and conscious entrepreneurs how to be better marketers" or Laura Roeder: "in love with small businesses using the web to take matters into their own hands".

Elinor Wilde, the "working mum's coach", has a Twitter profile that reads, "Is being a working mum a far cry from what you expected? I'm here to help you with the overwhelm and be the mum you want to be."

Yours might read, "I help pregnant women make empowered nutritional choices" or "Having your first baby at home? I'm your Edinburgh doula".

Think of your social media interactions as pathways to your main online home – usually your website. Interact with people on social media, but also direct them to this home.

Use a similar call to action as you would on your business cards. It's going to work even more effectively here because the person being asked to take action is already online. If they met you in person and got your card, they'd have to go home, sit at their computer and type in your URL (presuming they haven't lost your card en route) whereas when you link to your site from social media, potential clients are only a click away from your website.

You can spot your Tribe a mile off (and vice versa)

It's easy to waste time on social media so instead, get strategic.

Soon, if not already, you'll know your Tribe so well that you can spot them immediately. Focus your online energies on those people who are obviously your Tribe or who know your Tribe.

Through your profile, status updates and interactions with your connections, position yourself as the guardian angel of your Tribe. Demonstrate your expertise by showing up with useful comments and links. You'll become associated with who you serve and the challenges you can solve.

Forums

As with social media, demonstrate your expertise within a certain community.

One of the main ways my clients find me is through the Coactive Network which is an online forum for coaches who, like me, trained with the Coaches Training Institute (CTI). When I started as a new coach, I found the forum a great place to ask questions of more experienced coaches. These days, I jump in and help when I see a question about how to find clients. I include a standard signature every time that includes my photo, a link to my website and a call to action to subscribe to my newsletter.

Find forums where people might need you. Keep an eye out for frustration: what questions get asked that no-one else seems to answer adequately? That's a good indicator that your input is what's missing, so help out. See it as your duty to stop your beloved Tribe from going round in circles.

Articles and talks

Writing and speaking can both be effective ways of broadcasting your message.

Which is your preference?

Which might suit your Tribe better?

If your Tribe's situation is intensely personal or potentially taboo, it might be easier for them to read your article in the comfort of their own home, snuggled on their sofa, rather than having to attend a live event. On the other hand, they might feel safer meeting you in the flesh before deciding to work with you.

When making these decisions, think about which method allows you to show up in your brilliance, and which method allows your Tribe to feel most comfortable with you.

But so many magazines...

When deciding where to pitch an article or talk, ask the key question: will this reach my Tribe?

Find out which magazines, newspapers and newsletters your Tribe read. Find out which groups they're part of and which events they attend. Then use your time wisely and target only those publications and live events.

I wrote a regular column for the Cambridge Evening News business section that brought no evident interest so I stopped. I wrote one article for Om Yoga Lifestyle magazine and got an immediate sign-up to my programme, so I started writing a column for Om that brings in a steady flow of newsletter sign-ups each month. Monitor the success of your efforts and adjust your plan accordingly.

If you're writing an article, be sure to include your call to action, either within the article itself, or as a footnote, or ask the editor to include it in the contributors section. If you're giving a talk, get permission from the organizer to hand out a sheet so people can leave their email address and join your mailing list.

Video

It's also possible to become visible through online video sharing, for example using YouTube. Video provides a fantastic way for your Tribe to check you out "in person" from the comfort of their own home. My final reassurance for hiring Steve, the editor of this book, was seeing an interview with him on YouTube; he came across as warm, knowledgeable, professional and fun to work with. I doubt I'd have paid someone on a different continent if I hadn't had that connection.

Make your videos short, demonstrate your expertise, and give a call to action. Check out the examples on my YouTube channel (see Links and Resources).

There's an added bonus in that Google now owns YouTube so choose your titles and keywords wisely and you'll find yourself ranking highly. Think like your client. Search online as if you were them – what phrases do you type in? (For example, "working mum guilt", "help with my back pain" or "tired all the time".) If no video shows up in the search results, record one! Use that key phrase in the title and you'll quickly get found by your Tribe.

Remember, with every marketing method, you're associating yourself with your Tribe, with their challenges, with the most effective solutions, and with the message that you're the right person to offer those solutions.

Hold them

Once someone has visited your website, or whatever your main home is, make sure they feel welcome enough to stay a while – and come back again.

Imagine someone is running around like a headless chicken, trying to solve their challenges and the door to your home is open. You say, "Come on in" and you hold them in this way, offering relief and support.

You want to be able to keep communicating your message with them once they've left because they won't resolve their situation with one cursory visit. It's your duty to ensure they're no longer alone with their challenges.

This is where a *mailing list* comes in. A mailing list is a database of the names and email addresses of people who want you to stay in touch with them. By signing up to your list, they're giving you permission to send regular communications.

A mailing list gives you momentum when releasing a new service or product. You don't have to keep going back to square one each time, scanning your address book and wondering, "Now, who shall I tell about this?"

For the first few years in business, I had a little form on my website that people could choose to fill out with their name and e-mail address if they wanted to subscribe to my mailing list. I'd then go into my Gmail account and add their information manually to my "Newsletter" list.

It worked for a while – and you could start this way – but there are two problems with this approach:

Firstly, beyond a certain number of people, it becomes unwieldy. Your e-mail provider may limit how many people you can send an e-mail to, so when my list reached 500, I couldn't send an email out to the whole group at once. Instead, I had to divide the list up and send the message in batches. This would then put my Gmail account out of action for 24 hours, as I'd reached its capacity. It's massively time-consuming to divide your list and inconvenient to be without email for a day.

Secondly – and most importantly – this is not true *permission marketing*. You've added someone to your list but they haven't confirmed that they want to receive your emails. There's no way for them to automatically unsubscribe; they'd have to email you directly and ask you to remove them, which doesn't feel good for them, or you. If you don't have a *confirmed opt-in system*, you may find yourself holding back from sending emails, or from going full-throttle in your marketing communications.

So, as soon as possible, switch to a professional list management system (see Links and Resources). These services aren't expensive and they resolve the two problems so it's definitely a worthwhile business investment.

Here are some of the features these services offer:

1 – Subscribing and unsubscribing is automatic. Your Tribe have total control over whether they want to receive your emails or not. It's less awkward and more empowering to click a button saying "unsubscribe" than having to email you to ask. (And you do want people to unsubscribe – it's healthy to have a flow of new people coming on to your list, and others departing.)

2 – You can set up autoresponders. When I operated my list from within Gmail, I would reply personally to each new person who subscribed: "Oh hi Annie, delighted you signed up, I hope you enjoy it." This is fine for the first dozen people, but unfeasible when you start getting hundreds of subscribers!

Now I have autoresponders set up so when someone subscribes, they automatically receive an email saying "Thanks!" and confirming how often they'll hear from me. They then receive an autoresponder two months later, inviting them to email me and let me know a little more about them. Automating means you can mirror the one-to-one emails you'd naturally have with your Tribe on a larger scale.

3 – Personalization. Although you're broadcasting to many, you can personalize your emails so they include the person's first name in the e-mail. Your Tribe probably know that's part of the set-up, and that's fine and good – you're not trying to trick anyone into thinking you're sending individual emails – but I find it has a nice feel and is a reminder that you're writing emails with one person in mind.

How the mailing list process works

Once you've set up a list in your system, you'll receive a snippet of code that allows you to put a sign-up box on your website. When one of your Tribe enters their name and email address in this box, they'll receive an autoresponder from you, asking them to confirm that they want to receive these emails. This is called confirmed opt-in because the subscriber has to confirm twice that they want to receive your emails.

This is different from adding someone to your Outlook or Hotmail contact list simply because you collected their business card. That would be considered *spam*.

With confirmed opt-in, they've given you permission to email them relevant content. You can therefore quieten that inner voice that tells you, "Don't intrude in their life, don't pester them." You're completely free to tell people about what you're offering; you don't have to hold back.

Once you've got a list, you can determine a schedule for sending emails. You then write your message using the list management software, which sends that email out to your list and the emails will look like they've come from your email address.

Growing your list

Within a single account, you can set up different lists. You'll have your main database list which you can invite people to sign up to directly and you can also set up specific lists that feed people into that main database. One list might be for when people sign up for a free report or download.

I lead *free public teleclasses* every few months and people who sign up for those events can then join my main database list. A teleclass is an easy and effective way of communicating your marketing message and inspiring people to join your mailing list. You can showcase your expertise and help your Tribe. (The same is true of a *webinar* which is a web-based seminar, a way of sharing a slideshow as well as your voice.)

Here's how you'd set one up:

- **Choose your topic: a key concern or question that your Tribe would be hungry to hear answered. For example, a relationship coach might choose *Five Easy Ways To Pre-empt And Diffuse A Money Argument*.**

- **Invite people to sign up (use your email list, mention it on social media, ask people to spread the word).**

- **Email the dial-in number and access code to those who've signed up.**

- **Write your content.**

- **Dial in yourself and lead the class!**

Why teach a class?

Leading a teleclass or webinar is easier, logistically, than giving an in-person talk. You can do it from your home, in your pyjamas, with a script or notes in hand. Likewise, it's easier for your Tribe: they don't have to go anywhere, they can stay in their pyjamas. It's low-commitment for them.

The bonus factor is that you can choose a teleconference provider that records the call and makes it available to you as an MP3 recording. You can then email this to those people who registered but couldn't attend live, or you can publish it on your website as an additional resource, or you could turn it into a free giveaway when people sign up for your newsletter.

Still scary?

The first time I led a teleclass, I shook from head to toe. I was horrifically nervous. You might be too.

Now, when I lead a class, it feels normal and natural, like I'm phoning in to chat with a group of friends. It's lovely to connect with your Tribe without them having to pay you anything. It offers a more intimate form of engagement than written blog posts or videos allow and your Tribe can hear the voices of others in their community and feel less alone.

Billy no mates

Are you worried no-one will turn up? If you don't have a mailing list yet, don't let that hold you back. Kate led a teleclass and one person turned up – her mum. It didn't bother her, she did the call as if it were to a hundred people and then offered the audio recording as a valuable resource for her Tribe. She grew in confidence, grew her list, and her classes are now heavily subscribed.

Be aware of the 10% rule: for every 100 people who register for your teleclass, about ten will attend live. Don't let this deter you. This is fine, the other 90 people may listen to the recording in their own time – and anyway, you got to help ten people. Don't underestimate the value of starting small; it's where everyone starts.

Are you certain your Tribe wouldn't like the teleclass or webinar medium? Then don't use these methods. If it's not going to work for your Tribe, it's not an effective marketing method.

Other ways of growing your list

When I speak or lead a workshop, I pass around a sheet of paper at the end so people can add their name and email address. The next day, my assistant adds the names to my system. Those people then need to click a confirmation link within an email they receive so it's still permission marketing.

Start working on this now so you can build a list of people who *want* you to communicate with them. Over time, with a strategic approach, you'll grow your list until it's full of people who are interested in your approach and the services you offer.

Deciding on content

One popular approach to a mailing list is to email valuable content on a regular basis and then send out promotional messages with strong calls to action when you launch a new product or service.

Choose topics your Tribe will find genuinely useful. Use each email to remind your Tribe about the situations you help with and the services and products you offer.

> ***Make a list now of the main challenges you've heard – from research and with existing clients.***

If your Tribe's core challenge is "feeling stuck", you could create content like: *Three Quick Ways To Get Unstuck*, or *Why Feeling Stuck Could Be Good For You*.

Use your Tribe's words. For example, one of my blogs was entitled *Self-Employed Women Can't Afford To Get Sick* because I'd heard this concern from a client who used that exact phrase.

Rather than jumping around on lots of different topics, narrow your focus to the different facets of what it's like to be your Tribe. Let's say you're all about helping people find purpose in life. One facet of this might be "having a partner who's not supportive of your pursuit". One might be "feeling blocked around the money aspect". One might be "what if your purpose changes throughout your life?" One might be "common fears that stop us from finding our purpose", and so on.

Every single research interview will give you at least two or three topics to cover. If you intend to publish one blog or newsletter per month, that gives you a plan for two or three months of newsletters!

Go for the jugular each time. Find ways of repeating your core message. Here are a few titles my subscribers have found hit the spot: *Why I'm Glad You Hate Marketing, How To Promote Yourself Without Spending A Fortune, The Real Reason You're Scared, The One Non-Negotiable In Business*, and *Why It's Hard To Find Clients*.

Whatever mailing list format you choose, it's fundamentally a way to stay in touch with your Tribe, showing your expertise in understanding their needs. A mailing list means you're never far away when one of your Tribe needs support. It makes you familiar and accessible. Your Tribe can contact you by replying to your latest broadcast, writing, "Your email reminded me... I wanted to get in touch about..." How easy is that?

Any format

You can publish blog posts on your website (a WordPress site is technically a *blogsite* so the blog is integrated) and then link to them in your broadcast emails. These might include top tips or case studies. You could use pictures or audio or upload video blogs (*vlogs*) to YouTube and broadcast new uploads to your mailing list.

The Real Bread organization ran a free demo workshop at an event that was frequented by lots of their ideal clients: ethically-aware, eco-responsible London citizens. First, they handed out a bag of supermarket bread and, as we tasted the bread, they asked, "How does it taste?" and then spoke about the ingredients in it that are likely to give us headaches. This is marketing message Stage 1.

As we were unhappily chewing, they continued, "You may have realized that this bread doesn't taste good and you've tried to bake your own batches at home." Stage 2.

They then explained why our home-baking attempts might have gone wrong: "What was missing was you didn't know the length of time it took to allow the bread to rise." Stage 3.

"What you need instead..." they continued. Stage 4.

You might decide to demo your services at live events like this. Or perhaps you'll create a slideshow and add a voiceover, speaking your marketing message over the images, and then upload that as a video on YouTube. Amanda, with her logos for soul-led business owners, could find this an effective medium to demonstrate the difference between conventional business logos and the intuitive process she uses to create them. I recently came across a video on YouTube called "What? No Anesthetic?" which showcases a hypnotherapist who helped her client to undergo wisdom tooth extraction with no local analgesia.

If there's a tangible product involved, like Madeleine and her herb-growing kits for children, one of your strongest methods might be to have a stall at a fair, festival or conference. Madeleine's presence at eco-fairs and parenting exhibitions would give parents and grandparents a hands-on experience with the herb-growing kits.

When I bought voice recognition software, it was because I saw an online video demo that helped me imagine what it would be like to use.

What part of your process could you demonstrate?

You might record a video of your yoga class, cooking workshop or massage. A proofreader might take a screenshot of text before she's proofread it and a screenshot of the finished text. Could you explain your process with a step-by-step diagram?

Find something that enables your prospective clients to say, "Ah yes, I see how that could work!" The nature of your services will lead you to the most appropriate media.

▶ Ready for action?

In this step, I've scratched the surface of a variety of methods so you have a sense of the menu. Just as in a restaurant, you'd feel sick if you tried to eat everything. Don't feel you have to try all the methods at once. Instead, notice where you're feeling drawn.

> *Which methods would you like to explore first?*
>
> *Which feel most appealing to you and most relevant to your Tribe?*

Choose methods where you get to communicate in your most natural ways, and that match how your Tribe like to access information.

Before putting effort into any method, ask yourself three questions.

Question 1 – Does it suit you?

> *Does this feel like a way you'd naturally communicate?*
>
> *Does it play to your strengths?*
>
> *Does it give you the chance to express your most engaging qualities?*

One of the business mentors I follow writes beautifully. I'm totally engaged, hanging off his every word. It's an effective method because his blog posts are intimate and soul-to-soul and I want time to digest his information.

However, when he started experimenting with video in his marketing, I felt less connection. Now it might be exciting for him to develop a video marketing component, but as one of his Tribe, I think there are more engaging methods to explore. His voice over a slideshow might work better than the "talking head" approach and would still give him something to upload to YouTube.

I've received feedback that my Facebook profile is more engaging than my website because my Tribe see me interacting, creating community, talking about green smoothie recipes and the yoga or Five Rhythms class I went to. My Facebook profile has a vivacity and intimacy that a website doesn't.

So before deciding on a method, make sure it allows your natural strengths to shine through.

Question 2 – Does it suit them?

> *Does this method meet your Tribe in their preferred hang-outs?*
>
> *Is this a medium through which they like to receive communication?*
>
> *Does it create a high level of safety for them?*

Again, look to your research for the answers. Just as your marketing message is useless if it stays only on your computer, there's no point going crazy over Twitter if your Tribe have no clue what Twitter is. It may be that a magazine article or newsletter feature is more likely to reach them.

Remember: it's only an effective marketing method if your ideal clients receive the message.

Question 3 – Does it suit the service?

> *How does this relate to how the service is ultimately delivered?*

I've found that live events are effective for enrolling people in workshops because your Tribe get to meet you in person and there's no great leap between that and imagining themselves in a different room with you, enjoying your workshop. There's a feeling of safety because they can see what they're going to get.

A blog alone is unlikely to get you a steady stream of one-to-one clients for deep, transformative work. They need more of a feel for you than words on a screen typically offer. Video, live events and audio can bridge that gap, allowing your Tribe to get nearer to you.

Short-list

Go back through this step and circle the three methods you feel would be the most enjoyable and effective. Similarly, be brutal in crossing out the methods that are less of a match.

Now, look at those methods you've circled. Take action with one of them. If you already have a website, you might decide to set up a mailing list. Or maybe you don't want to create a website but know you need some online presence, so a Facebook Page or simple blog is your first method. Are you eager to speak? If so, make a list of local groups you could contact about giving a talk. Does it feel like you're meeting lots of new contacts but don't have a reliable way of staying in touch? Perhaps it's time to order those business cards.

Whatever you choose, above all, enjoy it! This should not be stressful or a chore. Keep it simple, keep it fun. You've been communicating with people for years. This is simply an extension of that, so consider how you naturally spread the word about things you believe in, things you think people should know about.

Bring to mind real-life instances when you've spread the word. Did you send out an email blast, throw an event, make it your Facebook status, blog about it or speak about it with everyone you met?

Marketing your business is no different. You're simply getting to hang out and communicate with your Tribe because you have something cool you want to share.

Let's check in

Here's what you might have spotted in Step Six:

- **That certain marketing methods turn you on and certain methods turn you off**

- **That there is a multitude of marketing methods and you will never be able to do them all**

- **That you have permission to market exclusively in the ways you and your Tribe will love**

Take a moment to gather up what you're taking from this step. Have you captured everything you want to? I invite you to reflect and make notes about your insights this far.

And let's check out

- You know the importance of Connection

- You know the importance of defining and claiming your Tribe

- You know how to do heart-to-heart research

- You know how to package your passion and stand confidently behind your price

- You know the message you want to communicate

- You know how to get in contact with your beloved Tribe

It's now time to look at the final stage of this journey. It's time to answer the question: how do you take strangers right through to becoming happy paying clients?

Let's move on to trouble-shoot your Flow.

Step Seven
Flow

Step Seven – Flow

This step will enable you to:

- **Create clear pathways to take strangers through to becoming paying clients**

- **Decide how to use technology to create smooth business processes**

- **Strengthen your way of reassuring clients they've made the right decision to work with you**

You've reached the final step. Congratulations for getting this far!

Hopefully you're starting to feel like you have a solid foundation for marketing your business. You've read a lot. Some information will have sunk in deeply; some will have tickled away at the surface.

Take a moment to notice how connected you are right now. Do you feel tuned in, or do you want to revisit your practice to get more connected? Do so now, if necessary. Make yourself as present as possible for this final, important step.

Know how

I'm imagining you starting to Do Marketing. You're putting your package together, crafting your message and telling people about what you do. But what if no-one's biting? What if people you interact with seem interested but aren't doing anything about it?

You're broadcasting, like a radio station, but no-one's phoning in and certainly no-one's coming in. It's as if there are no phone lines and no doors. You're working hard but have little to show for it.

You have the core marketing know-how but you may not yet know how your prospective clients will literally make their way to you. You don't know the doors and phone lines that go in to your business.

Ask yourself this question:

> *What actually happens when someone is interested?*

Blocked

There are often obvious blockages along the Flow that moves someone from complete stranger to happy paying client. That's what you'll be able to remedy after exploring this step.

You may have noticed internal blocks as you've worked through these previous six steps. You may be fearful of failure or of success; fearful of being visible or of change; fearful of having real-life clients to work with.

These fears can create blocks in your business Flow and need to be addressed. We're looking at a different type of block here, though – the one that occurs when you lack clarity around this question:

> *What happens once a prospective client has encountered your marketing message?*

Handling interest

Let's say you meet someone at a party. You start talking about what you do and after a while, your companion says, "Wow, this all sounds great!"

> *What do you do?*

It might come as such a surprise that you stumble over a response. "Oh! Uh, okay, um…" Before now, you might not have found people were captured by what you were saying so you didn't need to think too deeply about how to follow up on their interest.

But now you're getting good at communicating how you're a solution to your Tribe's needs. You're finding that people are engaging in those conversations with you, or reading to the very end of your webpage and wanting to take a next step.

Don't throw away their interest

I'm a dream client. When I want to hire a coach, get a massage or have acupuncture, I'm active in finding the right person and I'm very willing to pay.

Far too often, though, I'll reach a certain stage of conversation with a service professional and they'll say, "Oh great, you're interested, call me!"

This is a cavalier approach that is not good for me and not good for the professional. It's one of my pet peeves.

When you respond to a prospective client in this throw-away fashion, you are essentially abandoning them. They don't have a tangible next step to take in order to help themselves out of their situation.

If they want you, they'll find you – right?

Liz, a new coach said, "I met this guy, he seemed like a prospective client, he said he was going to call me, but he didn't. If he really wanted to work with me, he'd ring me, right?"

Have you noticed yourself thinking like this? That if they're not phoning you, they're not really interested?

It's true that sometimes when people say they're interested, they're just being polite. However, a lot of the time, they are genuinely interested but don't know what they're meant to do next. They're busy, they're in need – and so when you give them a general throw-away instruction like "phone me", it can be daunting. You're not giving your potential client enough sense of being held, of going from a place of vague interest to moving closer to getting support.

They should try harder

Kathy, a Tai Chi teacher, confessed to feeling snobbish about this. "I'm good, people should recognize I'm good and find me. They should find ways of getting in touch; I shouldn't have to work so hard!"

> *Have you ever thought this way?*
>
> *Should your prospective clients be making more of an effort to get in touch with you?*

Get curious about what impact this way of thinking has on your business. Consider reframing the sales process as an opportunity to serve your Tribe. You can start making their life easier from the first moment they encounter you.

And when you do this, you can expect to see a significant impact on your client and income level.

Call to action: the sequel

In Step Five, we looked at how to complete your marketing message with a clear call to action. This is the very first action that your prospective client would take, in order to work with you.

We now move to the sequel. What comes after that initial action step?

Think like a client

One of my most beloved business phrases is "Think Client" – in other words, think as if you were one of your prospective clients.

Literally, spend an hour being your potential client. Visit your own website (or other online presence) with the eyes of someone in your Tribe and be acutely aware of what the process is like for them.

Which page catches their attention first? What do they read? What do they click? What do they do next? Consider the step-by-step process from their point of view.

And then think about what happens before they find your site. How do they first hear of you? What happens after they've left your site?

You want to get a sense of the path they take, the Flow that enables a total stranger to encounter you for the first time, make initial contact, evaluate their readiness to get support, and ultimately decide to become your paying client.

There are more phases in that process than you'd think and if you're not clear what they are, it's a bumpy ride for others. And, understandably, people tend to want to get off a bumpy ride. It's uncomfortable. When a process is bumpy, then the sensitive aspects – like asking for commitment and payment – stand out more awkwardly.

Find your own Flow

To get a sense of your unique business Flow, it's time again to tap in to you, the storyteller. You're going to make up a story of how someone might go from total stranger to paying client.

Imagine a member of your Tribe, out there in the world, getting on with their own life. Then, they encounter your work. How do they hear about you? What do they do first? And next? Make it up, using previous client experiences or ideal scenarios.

You could turn this into a flow chart so you can visualize what happens if someone takes this path or another one instead. You'll become aware of the dead ends, the places where someone might drop out of engagement with you.

You might even decide to turn your Flow story into a game. One of the marketing coaches I mentioned in Step Five, Robert Middleton, talks about Marketing Ball, based on the baseball model. Your prospective client steps up to the plate and then moves through the next four bases, representing the different stages of engagement: stranger, vague interest, active interest, and so on. Working with this model in the earlier days of my business helped me think about the process from my prospective client's point of view – how would they first get in to the "game" with me, and how would they move forward?

Whether you see it as a game, a flow chart, or a step-by-step story, it's valuable to have a structure for thinking about your Flow. It gives you clarity and solidity, a much better place to be than vaguely wishing and hoping clients will find you somehow, somewhere.

Sharon's story

Here's one story of how a person might go from stranger to paying client. It's one example of many – and it's not a particularly dramatic story! – but notice how many different steps there are in the Flow:

1. On the train to work, Sharon (*a total stranger*) is reading Diva Magazine and sees a feature that mentions my website (*first encounter*).

2 Later in the office, on her lunch break, she remembers to get the magazine out of her bag and she types in the URL.

3. She browses the site.

4. She wants to let me know she enjoyed reading the feature and wonders if I might be able to help her, so she fills out the Contact form on my site and hits "Send" (this is *initial contact*).

5. The following day, she receives an email from me with a link to my online booking system (Tungle) and a note inviting her to a free 30-45 minute consultation, a chance for us to see if I'd be able to help.

6. She clicks the booking link and chooses her preferred time.

7. She receives confirmation from Tungle that the consultation is booked.

8. She receives an email from me double-confirming, with my phone number.

9. She writes the time and my number in her diary.

10. At the scheduled time, she calls (this is the *consultation*).

11. At the end of the consultation, she says it sounds like I offer the support she's looking for and so we diary in her first paid session then and there.

12. She receives a Getting Started email from me an hour or so later with our agreement, a payment link, and a client information form to fill out.

13. She clicks that payment link and sets up a recurrent monthly payment plan via PayPal.

14. She reads, initials and emails back the agreement.

15. She completes and emails back the client information form.

16. The following day, she receives an email from me confirming that the payment and paperwork have been received.

17. At the scheduled time, a week later, she has her first session (*becoming a paying client*).

> **What do you notice about that Flow? Pause here and consider.**

That's a lot of steps!

When I teach this module on the *Turn Your Passion To Profit* programme, participants are often stunned that there are so many steps. It's actually one of the shortest possible stories of Flow from stranger to paying client for my business.

It takes a while to put a Flow like this in place. There's technology involved: a website, a contact form, an online booking system and PayPal – and these might form part of the long-term infrastructure you build for your own business. I've worked with over a hundred long-term coaching clients so this system has been developed and streamlined over time.

Yours might start off with less technology, but it will still involve a number of steps. Once you put a Flow in place, you'll then develop and tweak it as you go forward so that it gets easier for you and easier for your prospective clients to work with you.

There are plenty of free and low-cost technical tools out there that can make your business life easier, once you've mastered them. With these systems in place, you'll have a relatively automatic set-up that doesn't take much input from you. It will be easier to enrol clients, because you're not starting from scratch each time.

However, in the meantime, you can still have a solid Flow from stranger to paying client without relying on technical systems. Sonia Calvo is getting her coaching business off the ground, supporting mums. While she waited for her website to be developed, her Flow looked like this:

Amy (*total stranger*) hears about Sonia from her friend, Joanna, who gives Amy Sonia's phone number. Amy calls Sonia (*initial contact*). She gets through to her voicemail which invites her to leave a message and her number. Later that evening, Sonia calls Amy back. They speak for thirty minutes (*consultation*). Amy is keen to go ahead with Sonia's three month coaching package so Sonia books their first session in her diary and emails over a summary of their conversation. She also invoices Amy and gives her two options for payment: she could either post three cheques (post-dated the first of each month they'll be coaching together) to reach Sonia in advance of their first session, or she could set up a standing order for three months. Amy opts for the latter (*becomes a paying client*).

There are so many places in this Flow where a glitch could occur. If Sonia's voicemail isn't warm and welcoming, if she doesn't explicitly ask the caller to leave a message and number, if she doesn't know how she expects someone to pay – all of these could create gaps in the all-important process. But because Sonia has thought through her Flow, it's a breeze for her and her prospective client.

An easy client?

Sharon and Amy knew what they wanted. They didn't ask to wait a few days to think about it.

But if they had, it would simply have involved a few more steps. At the end of the consultation, if Sharon had been unsure, I'd have asked, "What is it specifically that you want to think about? Do you need to check your finances, or speak with your partner?" We would then have made a note in our diaries to check back in on a specific date, once she'd decided what support was right for her.

Even if someone ultimately decides not to work with, you can still take a stand for them getting the right support for their situation – and if they choose to work with another practitioner, that's still a positive result for you.

I know that's hard to imagine when you're wondering where your rent or mortgage money is coming from, and that's why Connection is so important. It helps you remain trusting, and it also keeps you open-minded and resourceful. You might decide you want the relative security of a full- or part-time job while you grow your business; I did for the first few years, because I wanted to be discerning about who I was best placed to help, rather than chasing anyone who so much as looked my way.

There's no shame in having another stream of income while you build your own venture; in fact, it often helps you maintain your integrity. You can feel safe that you're being financially responsible and you don't need to cling to prospective clients.

The main reason why Sharon is an easy example, though, is that I've got my Flow down to a no-brainer process. It's easy for my prospective client. She doesn't have to think about where to go or what to do. I've taken all the hard work out and she doesn't have to make any decision other than, "Does this support feel right?" She steps into my Flow and is carried right through to that decision point. It's liberating for her and she feels reassured that she's walking a well-trodden path.

The power of decision remains in your prospective client's hands. She could say yes on the consultation and sound very keen, and then decide later that it wasn't the right choice. There should, of course, never be a sense of coercion. You're not making it easy because you want to cunningly manipulate her into commitment. You're making it safe and easy to say yes if that's what is right for her.

One great way of reassuring your prospective client (and yourself) that there are no sly marketing techniques at work is to offer a money-back guarantee on your services, ensuring that it's conditional upon your client putting in the required effort at their end. I include a no-risk, wise-investment guarantee on every service I offer which takes the pressure off the decision moment.

It's all in the timing – or is it?

In this particular example, there weren't any long lags in time.

By having a clear step-by-step system in place, you avoid those time gaps where a prospective client can drift away, un-held by you. You avoid that awkward limbo land, where you haven't heard from them in a while and you're not sure about getting back in touch because you don't want to feel like you're pestering them. Instead, you've got a clear follow-up system that ensures there's always a next step.

However, I only check my email once or twice a day and occasionally I go away for a few days and don't check email at all. So please don't think you have to be glued to your computer, ready to shoot back a response the moment someone contacts you.

I've replied to people after a week's holiday who have happily become clients. Prospective clients will wait for you to respond within a reasonable time if they're serious about getting their needs met. Your email account might allow you to schedule an out-of-office auto-responder which reassures prospective clients about when they can expect to hear from you.

How's your conveyor belt?

Let's imagine you're in a flapjack factory and there's a conveyor belt where the flapjacks trundle along. If a section of the belt went missing, the flapjacks would literally fall on the floor and be lost.

It's the same for your business. We want your Flow to be smooth, like a happily purring conveyor belt.

What pieces of your conveyor belt might be missing?

Once you know these possible gaps, you can take action to fix them.

Smooth shopping

Have you ever walked out of a shop because there was a gap in the shopping experience?

Have you tried to order something online and given up because it seemed complicated?

The term for this is an *abandoned cart*. It might be that someone changes their mind, but often it's because they don't know what to do next in the shopping process. We don't want this happening for your prospective client. It's your duty to help them along, step by step, to getting the support they crave.

If there's a physical shop or other building involved in your business, consider these questions:

> *How does a customer physically move around the space?*
>
> *How do they get to the till?*
>
> *How do they get their questions answered?*

If you have an online presence, check that someone can go from A to B to C without finding themselves at dead links and getting frustrated.

Get curious about where there might be gaps in your Flow. Look for ways to add a step or two to ensure the process moves smoothly.

Choose your own adventure

Did you read the *Choose Your Own Adventure* story books as a child? I loved them. You started on page one and then, after a few pages, you had to make a decision. If you choose to open the trap door, go to page 32. Or if you choose to run and hide, go to page 78. And so on, through the story, until you got to the sacred treasure, the pot of gold or some kind of victory. Or you went over the cliff, ran into a monster and met a brutal death. (You know, the kind a child loves!)

It's like this with Flow (minus the brutal death!). There are lots of variations, lots of different paths for your prospective client to choose. In my example, Sharon could just as easily have filled out the consultation form on my individual coaching page, or signed up for my newsletter, or gone to the blog page and left a comment.

There will always be lots of different options for your prospective client so just make sure that all roads lead to Rome. In other words, make sure that each option moves that person closer along the road to you and your support, so they always end up at your version of that "victory" page.

 When you give them your business card, don't just say "get in touch". Point out the email address and be specific: "When you get home, send me a quick email with the subject 'consultation' – you don't even need to write anything in the body of the email, I'll remember you – and I'll email you straight back with my online booking link."

However, business cards can sometimes be counterproductive because they add a step in to your Flow. You've met a prospective client at an event, they're interested and the next step is to book a consultation. So rather than giving them your business card, which adds distance, bring your prospective client closer. Get your diary out or say: "Write your email address down here and a general idea of the times you might be available to speak and I'll email you my online booking link when I get home."

Feel awkward?

You may have had negative experiences in the past of being hounded or manipulated by pushy and insistent sales people. You don't want to be like that so it's understandable that you might feel hesitant about guiding your prospective client into next steps.

I invite you to reframe what's happening here as helping your Tribe to get the support they need. Remember: you're not attached to the results. Your sense of safety is not conditional on how many clients you have. You're leaning in to Connection for your sense of security, not expecting it to come from them. If you make it easy for someone to get into a consultation with you, they might realize they don't need your help and instead find closure on an issue that has been bugging them for months, or even years.

You're in service

Clear calls to action and a smooth Flow are a public service. Your Tribe won't necessarily choose you for support, but they will have been helped in moving forward – and so you've been valuable to their journey.

Joy, the osteopath, understood this. She put a brilliant procedure in place: at the end of a session with a client, if they weren't sure whether they wanted another session, she'd offer to call them in two weeks to check in with them and schedule then, if appropriate. Her clients were delighted by this. One exclaimed, "Wow, you're like my secretary as well as my osteopath!"

As Joy shared this example with the other *Turn Your Passion To Profit* group participants, I had an image of her in a superhero outfit, flying through the sky to her clients, shouting, "Hang on, you said you wanted my help, I'm coming!"

It can be hard to get our own needs met. It can be hard to acknowledge that we're struggling, that we can't do everything on our own. Sometimes we don't feel safe enough to reach out. It's the same whether you need a cleaner, a massage therapist, an accountant, a counsellor or an illustrator. That's why you, as the practitioner, need to take those extra steps to reach out in return and make the process easy for the people who need your support.

Your pipeline

Once your business has a certain degree of momentum, you'll see that you have different people at each stage of your Flow – or of your *pipeline* as it's sometimes described.

Some people will have recently encountered you, others will be vaguely interested in your support, some will be about to sign the dotted line, and others will be satisfied paying clients, referring more people to you.

This is what makes your business sustainable. Your job is to keep your pipeline full – putting yourself in situations where you'll meet new people who can enter your Flow, and moving others step by step along the pipeline towards becoming paying clients.

Once you get to grips with that, you'll feel safe about the natural turnover in your business, rather than panicking that when one person completes as your client, you have to start all over again.

Someone could be on your mailing list, receiving your emails, for years before they make that initial contact. The seeds you're sowing now could produce fruit days, weeks, months or years from now. Your business Flow is a long-term investment.

Get strategic

As you get a sense of how full your Flow is and where people are in it, you can target your marketing activities at the most appropriate points.

If you're new to business, focus on bringing people in to your Flow. Soon, however, you'll find you have lots of people milling around at the "I know you and I'm a little bit interested" stage but they're not yet taking the next steps towards becoming paying clients. In this case, you'll want to focus your activities on moving people from interest to commitment. Perhaps your payment systems need to be streamlined, or you need to have more tangible calls to action in your blog posts.

The sales moment

What did you notice about the sales moment in my Flow? That part where commitment was made and money changed hands?

I'll bet you're having a hard time remembering it. This is because it was unremarkable. It simply had a natural place in the Flow, between someone being interested and someone starting work with me.

It wasn't personal. It wasn't me looking directly eye-to-eye at Sharon and saying, "I want you to pay me." It was simply, this is what happens at this point in the Flow. There was no fanfare, no break in the Flow.

Imagine you're out shopping for a new coat. You're browsing, you find one you think is perfect, you try it on, and it looks and feels fantastic. So you start walking towards the till.

Does an all-dancing crowd appear? Do neon lights flash? Does a banner drop from the ceiling announcing this is the Sales Moment?

No, of course not. It's not a moment that stands out. The shop assistants don't tense up and cling to each other as the customer approaches, whispering, "She wants to pay! What shall we do??!" Commitment to a purchase is expected; it's what most people who enter their shop intend to do.

Give safety

If people aren't saying yes to your offers, it can be tempting to panic and drop your price, assuming that you've chosen the wrong price point. However, if you've resonantly priced, and if this person is genuinely in your Love, Love, Money Tribe, then look to your Flow before you do any discounting.

When someone says no to your service, it is often because they don't feel safe enough to say yes. When you create a strong Flow, it conveys to your Tribe that there is a well-trodden path from stranger to paying client. This sense of safety will reassure them, quell some of those natural fears about taking a leap, and make it easier for them to say yes if that's the right choice for them. When someone feels safe, the money part of the process becomes much less of an issue.

Being clear on your Flow also helps you feel safer. You no longer need feel that your business activities are haphazard or random. You're in charge. You're guiding your clients down well-considered paths, getting the information you need about them and giving them the information they need. The whole process feels calmer to all those involved.

You get to decide for yourself how people should contact you, how they get to schedule time with you and how they need to pay you. It takes away that feeling that you're constantly putting out fires or that you're being bombarded from different angles by people asking for different concessions. You stand in your power as a business owner, as the creator of systems that work for you.

If you're like me, you crave clarity. Human interactions can be messy and if you're dealing with people and their emotions on a daily basis, it can be massively comforting and refreshing to lean in to clear logistical systems. They provide the structure within which you can do your deep and transformative work.

Four key phases

There are four main phases of Flow to hone in on. Your Tribe will be hanging out in any of these stages, in relation to you, with growing interest that eventually builds to the point of commitment.

These phases are:

- **Initial contact**
- **Some kind of consultation or scheduled conversation**
- **Commitment/payment**
- **Details beyond**

It's important to have systems in place for all four phases.

Phase 1 – Initial contact

This is the first time you hear from a prospective client. It's when they move from being something of a "stalker" – whether that's through checking out your website, watching you give a talk or reading an article you wrote – to actually telling you they're interested.

They might stay in the stalker phase for a few minutes or a few years – and then break free by commenting on your blog, sending you a tweet, leaving you a message on Facebook, emailing you, phoning your landline or mobile, texting you, approaching you at a party and saying, "I'm interested", or filling out a contact form on your website.

In this first moment of contact, they are putting themselves out there. They're taking a risk, even if relatively small. By reaching out to you, they're saying, "I have a need, I'm vulnerable." This is why it's so important to give them a structure for making that initial contact. You want to make it so easy for them to do this that they don't have to think about it. They can be reactive, rather than daringly proactive, and they can feel held and nurtured, rather than having to make tons of choices.

Forget email

Often new business owners put their email address on their website as the primary way they expect prospective clients to contact them.

There are two problems with this. Firstly, spam. As soon as your email address appears in hyperspace, the spam bots can find you and send you all kinds of Viagra and penis enlargement promotions. If you need that, great – put your email address up there so they can find you! If you don't, you can disguise your email address so that humans can read it, but not bots. Very simply, you'd type it like this: yes [at] youinspireme [dot] co [dot] uk so it's no longer recognizable by non-humans.

However, there's another reason why email isn't ideal. What on earth would someone say when they email you? If you hadn't contacted a colonic hydrotherapist, homeopath or ecstatic dance teacher before, would you know what to write? How long or short should your email be? What's too much information and what isn't enough? Will the other person think you're a pain, weird, or out of order?

Your prospective client will have question marks if the only instruction for getting in touch is "Email me." Sure, a few people might contact you this way but too many potential clients will be lost. They might procrastinate, they might be overcome with their gremlins saying, "She won't be interested in hearing from me with my little problems."

Even if they do sit down to write you that email, they probably won't give you the information you need. There are certain qualifying pieces of information you'll want to know before a prospective client can go to the next stage.

My recommendation is that you set up a simple way for people to make that initial contact: a *contact form*. By having one of these on your website, you make it a socially accepted process to fill out that form.

Just as in a restaurant, if there are jugs of tap water on the side, you know you're not going to be sneered at if you ask for tap water. Or if you go into any Apple store, you know it's okay to browse the internet because the computers are online and accessible and none of the sales assistants ask you not to. You can probably think of other businesses that make it socially acceptable for you to do something.

A contact form on your website, created either using the web software itself or an auxiliary provider such as EmailMeForm, provides a structured way for someone to contact you. When a person fills out that form, their input gets sent to your inbox. It's like having an online PO Box.

Which fields to include?

You get to choose the contact fields, thereby specifying the information you want from a prospective client. Focus only on what is most useful for the progression of your relationship together; don't turn the form into an obstacle.

Firstly, ask for the basic information you need: for example, name and contact details. I ask for an email address because I prefer to respond that way, but if you want to call them, then ask for their phone number. The forms that EmailMeForm offer allow you to check that an email address is valid, which is helpful in case your prospective client mis-types a letter or two.

You then want to ask qualifying questions. Don't waste their time (or yours) if it's not worth taking the interaction to the consultation stage. For the *Turn Your Passion To Profit* programme, these are my questions:

> *Briefly describe your emerging business (what you want to do, for whom, and why)*
>
> *What's the biggest challenge you face with developing your business?*
>
> *What would be possible for you if you overcame this challenge?*

The answers to these questions help me assess if a person could benefit from the programme. If she takes the time to fill out those fields, she is more likely to be committed to getting support.

You might then ask about their availability for consultation. For example, you might ask, "When is the best time for you to have an initial free conversation?" and you could give them a multiple choice tick box for Morning, Afternoon, Evening or Weekend. If your Tribe are international, ask for their time zone because "Morning" in Australia is substantially different from "Morning" in the UK!

Finally, include the field, "How did you find me?" It will only take someone one or two words to fill this out and it can be incredibly valuable for tracking marketing methods and their relative effectiveness. You also want to know if particular people are referring clients so you can shower them with gratitude.

There may be other fields that make sense for your particular line of work. Keep the form as short and sweet as you can but do ask for the information you want.

Serving them

Just as a good solution-to-pain marketing message can help your prospective client feel understood, a good contact form can help them to gain clarity. It can be useful for them to think through and respond to the questions you deem to be important at this stage of their journey.

Do you see how this whole marketing process is a service? You serve your Tribe through research, through your marketing message, through providing them with a structured contact form, and through having a consultation with them. And that's all before they become a paying client!

But some people hate forms...

It's important to have a few back-up options for people who don't want to fill out a form. There also might be a glitch with your form one day and you want other contact options available so someone can let you know.

What other contact options work for you? Are you comfortable making your landline or mobile number publicly available? Do you want to invite them to make contact on Facebook, Twitter, LinkedIn or by Skype? Would you like to include the disguised version of your email address?

Direct people to your preferred option but have a viable back-up option or two as well.

As you work through your Flow and visit your website thinking as client, ask yourself this question: how easy is it for someone to make initial contact? Test the contact form: is it easy to use? Does it work? Make sure you receive the input in your inbox and it's not going out into the ether! Eliminate any blocks that might be in the way.

Phase 2 – Consultation or scheduled conversation

Depending on your line of work, the consultation you offer in this stage might be free and without obligation – an opportunity to decide if you want to work together.

A consultation is not about you being assessed. The decision to work together is equally with both of you. Your primary question in a consultation is, "Can I genuinely help this person?"

In the coaching profession, there's a tendency to offer sample sessions. I'm not a fan. I offered these when I was starting out and felt I was constantly performing, giving all I could and then waiting to hear if someone wanted me or not. It was like an audition – and that's not a fun dynamic.

If you've tried the sample session approach and don't feel good about it, stop. Instead, think of this stage as a two-way process of listening to each other (mostly you listening to them!) and figuring out together if you're a match. Remember the curiosity and interest that guided your research? This is the perspective to employ here.

Here are some ingredients for a great consultation:

- **Give your prospective client space to describe their situation. If they've already given you some background information via the contact form, you can get to deeper aspects more swiftly**

- **As you listen for their needs, notice if you feel you can offer appropriate support. Gather all the information you require in order to authentically say either "Yes I can help you" or "You need to look around."**

- **Give your prospective client the chance to ask questions. They might want to clarify logistics or to know more about the theoretical basis of your approach. You might find it helpful to role-play this part with a friend or coach asking common questions so you feel confident you're able to answer from your heart. Return to Step Four if you don't yet feel confident about the details of what you're offering**

- **Now is the chance for you to sum up whether or not you feel there's a match. You can ask the prospective client: Does this feel like the right support for you? If they say yes, and you agree, then confirm that you'd love to work with them and explain where you go from here – in other words, what are the next tangible steps, once they've said yes?**

One coach said, "At the end of a sample session, I always insist they go away and experience at least two other coaches." She felt good about this because she believed it showed she was non-attached and that the decision was clearly in the other person's hands.

However, she was also struggling with her business, not having anywhere near the level of clients and income she wanted. Here's the flaw in her well-meaning approach:

Think back to the analogy of the coat shop. Imagine you've found the perfect coat. It was the first one you tried but you felt happy with it, you're clear about your decision, and you take it up to the till. When you get there, the shop assistant refuses to take your payment. Instead she says, "Okay, I know you like this coat, but I want you to go away and try on two more coats before deciding on this one." How would you feel, as the customer?

I'd feel uncomfortable, like I was being told I hadn't made the right decision (even though I'd been 100% sure before), and annoyed that the shop assistant wasn't on my side. She was pushing me back into the shopping phase, whereas I'd already left that phase and was ready to make my purchase.

Claim your Tribe

If I feel like I'm the right person for someone, I don't refer them elsewhere. I claim them and I declare, with certainty and humility, that I'm absolutely the right person to help them.

If I don't think we're a match, I wouldn't encourage them to shop around and come back to me. I'd stay in my integrity and say, "I'm not the right person for you." I'd hopefully be able to recommend a different coach or another practitioner who would be a good match.

It can be hard to let a prospective client go. This is where trust comes in. Trust that enough of your Tribe will come to you. Trust in the flow around you, that just as you refer your not-right people to others, they in turn will be referring their not-right people to you.

Let's move on to look at how you can receive money from your ideal clients.

Phase 3 – The commitment/payment

Mark Silver calls the sales moment the Sacred Moment. Have you experienced the sacredness of that moment, when a potential client says yes?

It's important to pause on this moment of your Flow long enough to witness it. Someone is opening their heart and saying yes to your help. It's an intimate exchange, an acknowledgement of interdependence between you.

Pause enough to witness it – and then you can naturally and smoothly move on to the commitment piece. This is where an agreement is signed, an invoice is honoured or a PayPal button is clicked. Payment is what anchors the commitment.

You might freak out at the mention of money so it's especially important to get clear on this part so it comes easily to you. You can stay in consultation mode, focusing on the needs of the person in front of you, without having to change gear. You don't suddenly have to pick up a different sales script.

Money will probably have come up when they ask questions; they might ask, "Remind me how much it is?" or "And how do I pay?"

Spend time considering how a person commits to your service or product. My yoga teacher, Rachel Hawes, emails a PayPal link so students can pre-pay a five-session package, which makes classes £1 cheaper than if we paid on a drop-in basis. Rick Lawrence, the designer of this book, divided his fee in quarters and sent an initial invoice for the first quarter, which I paid by bank transfer before he started work on the cover design. I recently enrolled in an improvisation drama course and was asked to pay the full fees up front by posting a cheque to the tutor's house.

What does the commitment part look like in your Flow?

How can you make it easy for someone to commit?

If your prospective client says they want to go away and think about it, ask this powerful question: "What would you need to know to be able to commit right now?" It's daring and you might feel uncomfortable asking it at first but it enables you to discover the prospective client's lingering fears or unanswered questions.

Is this the final stage? No. It's very important to consider:

Phase 4 – Beyond commitment/payment

There's a danger of losing the prospective client after they've said yes. They may backtrack on their commitment if it doesn't feel safe after the sales moment.

When I did a bungee jump in New Zealand, I paid my money, filled out the disclaimer forms, said yes, and stepped forward onto the ledge, metres and metres above a lake of crystal clear water. I was shaking with terror but I was committed.

However, if the team had started bungling up the cord or expressed any kind of uncertainty or confusion, I would have stepped away from the ledge!

It's the same here. Your new client is taking a leap with you. So make sure the details are clear and keep holding them right through from commitment to payment and then to that first paid connection with you.

What could you do between their "yes" and their actual experience of what they've paid for?

Generally, a new client will feel a mix of apprehension and eagerness to get going. You could send them a questionnaire, a checklist or an exercise to work with, to help them engage with the process immediately, while they're in that state of readiness. Help them to experience confirmation that they've made the right decision.

When a woman signs up for the *Turn Your Passion To Profit* group programme, I send her a Joining Information email right away that confirms the dates of our group calls so she can commit the time into her diary. It anchors the commitment, makes it real. I also send her an overview of the entire step-by-step journey so she can start looking forward to the structure, and I give her a number of free audio recordings that she can listen to as appetizers. These set the context and give her immediately actionable tips before the programme starts in full. In the month before the programme starts, she receives an email every week, introducing her to the other group members, building a sense of community and fuelling her excitement.

> ### What's your version of this?

▶ Ready for action?

Firstly, bring to mind a recent service you purchased, something with a similar financial investment to that which you are offering (for example, signing up for an organic vegetable box; a haircut; a holiday; a professional development programme).

> ### How was that Flow?
>
> ### Did it feel smooth or bumpy to go from stranger to paying customer?

"Think like a client" and write down each step you remember in that Flow.

Then, use any previous experiences you've had with your own paying clients or practice clients (as well as imaginary ideal scenarios) to generate at least three possible Flow scenarios for your service.

Write down these simple Flows; don't leave them in your head. Seeing the process in black and white makes it tangible and also enables you to see the missing links in the chain.

Share your Flow with someone. They may spot gaps where a prospective client could drop off your conveyor belt. They can also tell you where it feels like there's hassle involved.

Finally, think about the actions you need to take to ensure a smooth Flow. Do you want to create a contact form? Set up a PayPal account? Create a checklist or exercise for your new client to work with before their first paid encounter? Role-play the initial contact with your friend or coach?

Continue to be aware of your Flow on an ongoing basis. As you get to know your Tribe (and yourself), you'll be able to refine your Flow, making it as smooth as possible for a stranger to move towards you and become a happy paying client.

Let's check in

Here's what you might have spotted in Step Seven:

- **That your business has a conveyor belt and if there are missing sections, your prospective clients (who need you) will never get as far as booking their first session**

- **That you can build this infrastructure over time and use technology to assist you**

- **That it's vital to help your prospective client feel safe enough to say yes and stay committed**

Take a moment to gather up what you're taking from this step. Have you captured everything you want to? I invite you to reflect and make notes about your insights this far.

And let's check out

You now know so much.

- **You know the importance of Connection**

- **You know the importance of defining and claiming your Tribe**

- **You know how to do heart-to-heart research**

- **You know how to package your passion and stand confidently behind your price**

- **You know the message you want to communicate**

- **You know how to get in contact with your beloved Tribe**

- **You know how to create a smooth and seamless business Flow**

It's now time to review and celebrate!

Review and Celebrate

Review and Celebrate

Remember when you first opened this book.

What were your hopes?

What were your fears?

What mattered most?

Take a moment to consider where you are now.

What feels clearer, what feels easier?

What have you discovered about you, your Tribe and the nature of your unique business?

You might like to reflect and write about your journey, answering the questions above. Take time to let the impact of your experience register, as if you were at the top of a mountain, surveying how far you've come.

What did you expect this book would do for you and how has it turned out?

You may have physical evidence to look back on, scribbles of insights you had along the way. You may notice your brain feels subtly – or massively – different, as mindset shift after mindset shift has clinked and clunked.

You've come this far – and I am so glad. I loved putting this journey together for you and I celebrate you for being a finisher!

I would love to hear from you: what did you enjoy? What challenged you? What do you feel will make the biggest difference in how you approach your business?

Please get in touch. Email and let me know: *yes@youinspireme.co.uk*

And while you're in communication mode, email your friends – the ones who want to be successfully self-employed but don't yet know how to make a living doing what they love. Tell them to check out this resource and get a copy so that they, too, can take this journey.

Time for action

You're doing wonderful work and are now equipping yourself to be wonderful at the business side too. You are truly who I named my business for because You (do) Inspire Me.

You have chosen a brave path with self-employment, and by reading this book you have demonstrated your commitment to moving forward.

You have a lot of knowledge. You now know how to define who you work with, position yourself as a needs-based business, communicate authentically, and help people feel safe enough to say yes to working with you.

But knowledge is only fractionally useful if it stays in your mind. It's time to put into practice what you know. The days of being the world's best kept secret are over. It's time for you to become a beacon for your ideal clients, so that they can get helped and you can get paid.

You're full of passion and that precious energy will stagnate if you don't take action. It needs to be channelled, to benefit both you and the people you want to help.

You're undoubtedly going to get scared along the way. Those demons of self-doubt come running when you get on your path. Your fears are valid, but they cannot win. The people who need you are too important. It is your duty to get clarity about what you do and to communicate that with those you're here to serve. Remember: you have diamonds in your pocket.

You have not arrived at the edge of a cliff. You do not have to jump and close your eyes and pray that a net or parachute will appear. You don't have to lie staring at the ceiling, wondering, "How am I going to take this forward?"

You have options.

You can read this book again, engage step by step. If you feel you've gone as far as you can alone, you have other support options available, both from me and from others. You can move from solitary reading to shared journeying.

If you've felt aligned with my approach, then I'd love to welcome you to the next stage of support. Whether you'd prefer the group format of sharing experiences and insights with like-minded others, or you're craving tailor-made individual support, there's an option to suit you.

Get someone else's eyes on you and your business. Find others to celebrate with, to bounce ideas off, to hold you accountable and give you a kick up the backside when you need it. Don't let yourself wriggle away from implementing what you know will work. Your fledgling venture is too precious for that.

Visit: *www.youinspireme.co.uk/what-next*

This is the end of the beginning. As you progress from here, my heart's earnest desire is that you enjoy deep personal and professional fulfillment, turning your passion to profit.

Links and Resources

Links and Resources

Here are some of the people, companies, resources and services mentioned in each step.

Step One – Connection

The Findhorn Foundation   *www.findhorn.org*

Julia Cameron, author of *The Artist's Way*   *www.juliacameronlive.com*

Step Two – Tribe

Tad Hargraves   *www.marketingforhippies.com*

Naomi Dunford   *www.ittybiz.com*

Joanna Penn   *www.thecreativepenn.com*

Steve Parolini   *www.noveldoctor.com*

Step Three – Research

Professional online surveys, e.g.   *www.surveymonkey.com*

Step Four – Package and Price

Mark Silver and Jason Stein   *www.heartofbusiness.com*

Step Five – Message

Robert Middleton   *www.actionplan.com*

Suzanne Evans   *www.helpmorepeople.com*

Step Six – Methods

Email marketing software, e.g.	*www.aweber.com*
Adam Kayce, web developer	*www.brightcoconut.com*
Laura Roeder	*www.lauraroeder.com*
Telephone conferencing, e.g.	*www.conferencegenie.co.uk*
Online event tickets, e.g.	*www.eventbrite.co.uk*
Business cards, e.g.	*www.vistaprint.com, www.moo.com*
Online article directories, e.g.	*www.articlesbase.com, www.ezinearticles.com*
Blogging software, e.g.	*www.wordpress.org, www.wordpress.com, www.blogger.com*
YouTube, e.g.	*www.youtube.com/passiontoprofit*

Step Seven – Flow

Online booking system, e.g.	*www.tungle.com*
Email contact form, e.g.	*www.emailmeform.com*
Online payment, e.g.	*www.paypal.co.uk*

You're in good company

Here are some of the people whose shining examples have featured in this book.

Amanda Galati	*www.lovearttruth.com*
Audrie Reed	*www.beautifulmemories.tv*
Becca Harrison	*www.heretoshine.com*
Beth Follini	*www.ticktockcoaching.co.uk*
Claire Bradford	*www.facebook.com/straightforwardcoaching*
Claire Cordingley	*www.thomasinaj.blogspot.com*
Clodagh Beaty	*www.bigbluecoaching.com*
Denise Duffield-Thomas	*www.deniseduffieldthomas.com*

Gemma Gordon	*www.emeraldacupuncture.co.uk*
Elinor Wilde	*www.theworkingmumscoach.co.uk*
Joy Haughton	*www.abodythatworks.com*
Julie Shepherd	*www.inspiringlifechanges.co.uk*
Kris Carr	*www.crazysexylife.com*
Linda Anderson	*www.tapintoyoursuccess.co.uk*
Lorraine Burwood	*www.lorraineburwood.co.uk*
Louise de Caux	*www.simply-being.co.uk*
Madeleine Giddens	*www.madaboutherbs.com*
Margaret Hiley	*www.margarethiley.com*
Muriel Bauer	*www.murielbauer.com*
Nicola Marshall	*www.braveheartsolutions.co.uk*
Petra Schlitt	*www.petra-schlitt.de*
Polly Noble	*www.pollynoble.com*
Rachel Hawes	*www.massage-movement.co.uk*
Rick Lawrence, web & design	*www.samskara-design.com*
Rosanna Gordon	*www.rosannagordon.com*
Sonia Calvo	*www.creatingserenity.com*

Also: Jacqueline Beall, Leanne Callaby and Sandra Staley

Acknowledgements

At age 17, I was offered a place at Oxford University to read English. My family were proud, my teachers were excited; my grandma, a child refugee from Nazi Germany who'd missed out on opportunities and education, said she'd give her right leg and eyebrows for the chance to go.

I turned my place down. I was immersed in the passions of my first relationship and with teenage reckless abandon, I decided that following the person I was infatuated with to the university of *their* choice was more important.

In the years since, I have regretted that decision. But as I write the final words of this book, I feel the sense of being in exactly the right place, at exactly the right time and that no other path was necessary.

So, thank you to those of you who have made *Turn Your Passion To Profit* possible, whether by taking the journey yourself or by supporting me in putting it together in this form. You have helped me see that there is nothing to regret and that I am 100% on my right path.

Specifically, thank you to:

The pioneering *Turn Your Passion To Profit* groups (the Robins, Blackbirds and Nightingales) and to my individual coaching clients for allowing me to walk beside you, as a witness and companion for your inner and outer journeys.

Nick Kettles (author of *The All-Seeing Boy and the Blue Sky of Happiness*) and Nick Williams (author of *The Work You Were Born To Do*). You both spotted a spark in me when I was 1,000 miles behind you on the path and spoke to me as if I were next to you. You saw in me what I only dreamed was possible and your belief called me in to it.

My four powerful business support guys: Daniel Paterson, Jason Stein, Mark Silver, and Adam Kayce, and the book birthing gang: Jo Calam, Joanna Penn, Steve Parolini, Catherine Laurence, Rick Lawrence, and the team at MPG Biddles Limited.

My beloved family, for teaching me that happiness is what matters and that it's okay not to follow the rules, and to my best friends – Chu Askew, Beck Collins, Rosanna Gordon, Joey Clifton and James Southwick – for confirming that heart-following is allowed in adult life as well. (And James, an extra thank you for your piano compositions; what a beautiful soundtrack for writing this book.)

Sam, my light, my twin. I thank you for your unerring support, your love and for believing that I could do it – not just this book but the whole self-employment journey. You have given me both an anchor and wings and my smile is so bright because of you.

And finally, to *you*. Our world can be easier, more comfortable, more peaceful and more joyful – and you and your unique contribution can help make that happen. The world needs your passion; thank you for letting us have it.

About the Author

Corrina Gordon-Barnes, author of *Turn Your Passion To Profit*, is a certified professional co-active coach (CPCC), having trained with the Coach Training Institute (CTI).

Described by motivational speaker Anthony Robbins as "an articulate and passionate agent for change", her clients are women who care deeply about the world and want to make a difference, but don't yet know how to make that pay the bills. She is committed to ending chronic under-earning and under-serving in those who bravely choose to do what they love with their lives.

She was an early adopter of the self-employed lifestyle, earning money from baby-sitting and car-washing from age ten. She later worked for a local health authority, a radio station, a record company and HM Customs and Excise. She travelled the UK and Ireland as an educational tour manager, showing off historic places to teenagers from Hawaii and Rhode Island. She fundraised for Shelter, ran youth groups for gay, lesbian and bisexual teenagers and led homophobia-busting workshops in schools. She managed a backpackers' hostel in Brisbane, Australia and trained at Cambridge University as an English and Drama teacher.

She started her business, You Inspire Me, in 2005 and has served over one hundred individual coaching clients and hundreds more workshop and programme participants.

Her inspirational writing has been published in *Om Yoga and Lifestyle*, *Cambridge News, The London Paper, the Ecologist, Caduceus, Permaculture Magazine* and *The Vegan* and she was awarded the Ooffoo Laureate 2008 for her acclaimed piece, "The World Needs Your Passion".

She currently lives in Cambridge, England with her partner Sam.

Contact

Corrina Gordon-Barnes

yes@youinspireme.co.uk
www.youinspireme.co.uk

Tel: 01223 415113

Twitter: *www.twitter.com/CorrinaGB*

Facebook: *www.facebook.com/CorrinaGordonBarnes.YouInspireMe*